Florida's Megatrends

Florida A&M University, Tallahassee
Florida Atlantic University, Boca Raton
Florida Gulf Coast University, Ft. Myers
Florida International University, Miami
Florida State University, Tallahassee
University of Central Florida, Orlando
University of Florida, Gainesville
University of North Florida, Jacksonville
University of South Florida, Tampa
University of West Florida, Pensacola

Florida's Megatrends

Critical Issues in Florida

David R. Colburn and Lance deHaven-Smith

University Press of Florida

Gainesville · Tallahassee · Tampa · Boca Raton
Pensacola · Orlando · Miami · Jacksonville · Ft. Myers

07 06 05 04   6 5 4 3 2

LIBRARY OF CONGRESS CATALOGING-IN-PUBLICATION DATA
Colburn, David R.
Florida's megatrends: critical issues in Florida / David R. Colburn and
Lance deHaven-Smith.
p. cm.
Includes bibliographical references and index.
ISBN 0-8130-2532-X (pbk.: alk. paper)
1. Florida—Social conditions—20th century. I. deHaven-Smith, Lance.
II. Title.
HN79.F6 c65   2002
306'.09759'0904—dc21   2001054020

The University Press of Florida is the scholarly publishing agency
for the State University System of Florida, comprising Florida A&M
University, Florida Atlantic University, Florida Gulf Coast University,
Florida International University, Florida State University, University of
Central Florida, University of Florida, University of North Florida,
University of South Florida, and University of West Florida.

University Press of Florida
15 Northwest 15th Street
Gainesville, FL 32611–2079
http://www.upf.com

contact person is
angela   as@ upf.com

Contents

Photo sections follow pages 26, 61, and 115

Acknowledgments

We started discussing a book on the future of Florida shortly after we finished our previous book, *Government in the Sunshine State*. We were both looking for a project that gave us a chance to work together again (yes, there are a few Gators and Seminoles who are friends and colleagues) but one that also provided us with an opportunity to stretch beyond our respective fields of history and political science. What struck us from our work on *Government in the Sunshine State* was that there was a great deal of speculation about Florida's future, but not much of it reflected an understanding of the state's past or its social, economic, and political heritage. It was the absence of such a perspective that convinced us that this book was needed and could be helpful to Floridians and policy leaders as they seek solutions to problems that currently bedevil the state and promise to challenge its future.

In conversations with a few colleagues and our editors at the University Press of Florida, we decided to begin work on this project. In the end, the manuscript took longer to complete than we had envisioned, as is usually the case. But we never found this project boring, because it gave us an opportunity to stretch our thinking and to argue with one another about what it all meant for Florida's future. Moreover, the presidential election of 2000 came along as we were nearing the end of the book, and it rejuvenated both of us.

We may not have the story of Florida's future correct, but we believe this book will cause Floridians to think about their future and that of this great and fascinating state. We are sure that many people will disagree with us, and we welcome that criticism. Half the enjoyment of writing a book like this is to challenge people's thinking and to stir a little controversy. We would be disappointed, in fact, if this book does not do that.

There are a number of people who helped us frame our argument and polish the prose and content. We owe the following a special debt of gratitude in this regard: Jeffrey Adler, Gary Mormino, Susan Mac-Manus, Chuck Frazier, Cynthia Barnett, Michael Gannon, Jim Clark, Lynda Keever, Richard Scher, Jim Button, Jason Parker, Lynn Leverty, and Reubin Askew. We were fortunate, as always, to have some terrific editors at the University Press of Florida, particularly Judy Goffman, and Meredith Morris-Babb, and freelance copyeditor Polly Kummel. The press has become a great place for scholars to publish their work, and we thank Ken Scott, the director, for creating that environment.

We take particular pleasure in dedicating this book to our children and their future: Margaret Cauthon, David Colburn, Jr., Katherine Fulmer, Erin Crutchfield Smith, and Joseph deHaven-Smith

Photos not otherwise credited are courtesy of the Florida State Archives, Tallahassee.

Introduction

What a century! In 1900 most residents of Florida lived within fifty miles of the Georgia border in what was a rural, agricultural, and frontier-like society. Jacksonville was the largest city with 28,249 residents, and Pensacola stood a distant second with 17,747. Miami was a mere outpost with 1,681 residents. The Florida of 1900 was also racially segregated, with a one-party political system and an environment that seemed ill suited to development.

Yet during the next hundred years Florida evolved from the smallest state in the South, with slightly more than half a million residents, to become the largest, with nearly 16 million people (fig. 1). By the end of the twentieth century it was virtually unrecognizable as the state that it had been in 1900. Today Florida is the fourth largest state in the nation and the most urban in the South. Floridians are people of color and among the most racially and ethnically diverse in the nation. Tourism and construction dominate the state's economy, which is increasingly influenced by international commerce and technology. Agriculture remains prominent but substantially less so as each decade passes. Perhaps symbolically, the state is the launch site for future space explorations, and Miami serves as the gateway to the Caribbean and the financial and cultural capital of the region. Who in Florida would have imagined any of this in 1900 or even in 1940? In 1999 the *New York Times* called Florida one of the bellwether states for the twenty-first century as a result of these changes and those projected for the new millennium.[1]

Florida's modernization, however, has been neither easy nor complete. Intense political conflict, limited financial resources, environmental obstacles, regional divisions, and a general absence of a state-

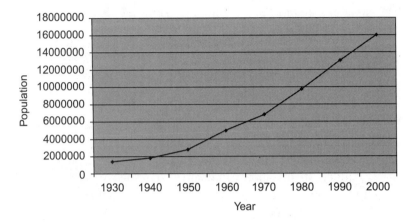

Fig. 1. Population of Florida, 1930–2000

wide identity have frustrated the state's struggle to emerge from its Old South traditionalism. If Florida is indeed a bellwether, and we think it is, we will see a tumultuous transition in the twenty-first century to a nation in which a majority of its population is aging and is more ethnically and racially diverse.

Florida's newfound importance nationally and internationally, and its lack of preparation for this position of influence, came to light all too clearly in the disputed 2000 presidential election. The political battle for Florida, perhaps more than any other event in its modern history, revealed the challenges that it faces. Moreover, many in the nation glimpsed their own future, as Florida's senior citizens, Hispanics, African Americans, and rural voters disputed the election process and the election outcome. Although Florida is very much a twenty-first century state, it found itself wrestling with twentieth-century institutions that had been heavily influenced by its pre–World War II politics and culture. The state's ability to bring its historic institutions and culture together with current economic and demographic realities will have a profound effect on its future.

In this book we will examine these megatrends and the ways that they have shaped Florida in the twentieth century. In addition, we project the trends for the state through the first quarter of the twenty-first century and discuss the implications that these developments have for Florida and Floridians.

The Reinvention of Florida in the Twentieth Century

No one in 1900 could have envisioned the Florida of 2000. At the beginning of the twentieth century, large areas of the state were literally uninhabited. Transportation was difficult, if not impossible, in many places, and those who came looking for paradise found the swamps, bugs, humidity, and absence of civilization more than they could tolerate. Residents who lived in and around the Everglades were, not surprisingly, an independent, self-reliant, and cantankerous lot. Outlaws occasionally fled to Florida, seeking refuge in the isolation of the Everglades and betting their freedom on the autonomous nature of local residents. Despite their prideful independence, Floridians yearned for the economic development and population growth that would enable them to prosper. The state Grange, an organization of Florida farmers, observed in its publication in the 1870s, "Unquestionably Florida's greatest need is immigration; next to immigration we need capital."[2] State politicians offered various incentives, from free land to low taxes, in an effort to attract newcomers and serious investors, but only a few took advantage of the opportunities. Visitors occasionally entered the state, but most returned home delighted to have escaped the bugs, heat, humidity, and primitive conditions of Florida.

As late as 1940 Florida remained the least populous state in the South with fewer than two million people. The state had expanded substantially in the previous forty years and had experienced a brief and dramatic boom in the 1920s that had, unfortunately, presaged a crushing depression. Despite the growth in population from 1900 to 1940, the development of the southeast coast, and the emergence of important cities in Tampa and Miami, Florida's political, social, and economic culture remained remarkably similar to what it had been at the turn of the century. The state remained a backward, rural, agricultural, and segregated society. All that would change, however, after 1940 with the onset of World War II in Europe and America's entry into the war.

Because of its geographic isolation from the rest of the nation and daunting environmental conditions, Florida seemed an unlikely place to experience much change in its population or in other aspects of its society as the war began, but the involvement of the United States and national mobilization would transform Florida forever. The federal government poured men, money, and matériel into the state, constructing naval and air bases in all regions of Florida. The arrival of military personnel, laborers to construct military bases, and the relatives of both groups helped to energize and reinvigorate the state economically from Miami to Tampa, Jacksonville, and Pensacola. The land boom of the 1920s paled in comparison to the war boom of the 1940s.

With the benefits of pesticides, which were first used during the war years, and the gradual introduction of air-conditioning in the late 1940s and 1950s, people flocked to Florida after World War II. Florida was the smallest state in the South in 1940, but by 1960, in the space of only twenty years, it had become the most populous below the Mason-Dixon line. Approximately 2.5 million people on average entered the state in each of the remaining five decades of the twentieth century. Many came initially as tourists; they returned as residents. The state made overtures to those who lived in other states in the form of low taxes, inexpensive land, economic opportunity, and radiant sunshine, all of which spurred the arrival of newcomers. Fifty years later, at the end of the twentieth century, people continued to stream into Florida at the phenomenal rate of 684 per day, but they now came not only from various points in the United States but from Canada, the Caribbean, and Central America as well.

What intrigues historians, demographers, and political scientists about Florida is the way in which it responds to the needs and concerns of its dynamic and divergent population and the way it creates one out of the many who choose to settle there. Florida has the second-largest percentage of senior citizens (beyond only West Virginia's) in the United States, with 18.5 percent, or more than 2.8 million people, older than sixty-five. Florida's retirement community in 1998 was in fact larger than the population of seventeen states in the United States. The immigration of people from the Caribbean and Central America also has given Florida an increasingly diverse population; they have been settling along the southeast coast and now constitute 16.8 percent of the population, of which Cuban Americans constitute half that number. Florida is one of six states, along with California, Texas, New York, New Jersey, and Illinois, that receives more than 90 percent of the immigrants, legal and illegal, who enter the United States each year. Projections for the twenty-first century are that Florida will continue to see dramatic increases in its immigrant population from the Americas. At 14.6 percent the state's African-American population is only slightly smaller than its Hispanic population. After declining throughout the twentieth century as a percentage of the total population, the African-American population also is expected to increase in the twenty-first century, to 17.17 percent by 2025.

What also makes Florida fascinating is that the regions of the state reflect in microcosm national trends and changes in national identity. Southeastern Florida increasingly serves as a vast ethnic and immigrant cauldron of people from throughout the Western Hemisphere. Miami is a financial metropolis that interacts daily with the Caribbean and South America and has a significant influence on this region of the world, both economically and culturally. Through its tourist industries and the megacorporation Walt Disney Company, Central Florida represents the appeal of traditional American values and a family-oriented lifestyle that many seek for themselves and friends. Significantly, more teenage runaways fled to Orlando in 1997 than any city in the United States, searching for the relationships and values, embodied by Disney World, that they hoped would give their lives support and meaning. In many ways northern Florida and the Panhandle still constitute the Old South, a region of Dixiecrats, lumber companies, farmers, and poor blacks struggling to secure an existence amid the challenges of nature, middling land, and steadily eroding lumber and farm prices. And areas of southwestern and southeastern Florida serve as havens for seniors who have sought to enjoy their penultimate years in the state's salubrious and nearly tax-free environment.

Florida is a place of unusual variety. And the way that it harmonizes this diversity, adjusts to the changes of the twenty-first century, and interfaces with the new world order of the twenty-first century is what stimulates so much interest in the state.

Florida's Distinctiveness and Identity Crisis

Florida's heritage extends back to its Native American and Spanish roots, although residents today encounter their influences largely through the names of cities, counties, rivers, and parks, its architecture, and the Seminoles' gambling operations. During the nineteenth century Florida abandoned much of its diverse heritage to become part of the Deep South, as settlers from nearby southern states streamed across its border in search of new and inexpensive land. To this day the state retains remnants of a southern culture in its northern and Panhandle areas and in a line that extends through the center of Florida from the Georgia border to the Everglades. By the middle decades of the twentieth century, migrations into the central and southern parts of the state had begun to separate Florida from its southern roots and link it closely to other Sunbelt states like California and Texas. Few other states have experienced such dramatic changes in their population and have had such diverse ethnic, racial, and regional influences.

Florida's political environment is also unique because of its extensive urban and regional diversity. Most states have one or two large cities that dominate or significantly influence state politics. Georgia, for example, has Atlanta, New York has New York City, Pennsylvania has Philadelphia and Pittsburgh, Massachusetts has Boston, and Illinois has Chicago. By contrast, Florida is an urban state, but it lacks a major urban center. Ninety-three percent of the state's population resides in twenty metropolitan areas that are scattered throughout its various regions. These cities include Jacksonville, Miami, Fort Lauderdale, Daytona Beach, Fort Myers, Orlando, Tampa, St. Petersburg, Pensacola, Gainesville, Tallahassee, and West Palm Beach. The geographic dispersion of these cities has fostered many political divisions in Florida as representatives seek political benefits for their community and their region, often at the expense of others.

These characteristics combine to make twentieth-century Florida a colorful, complex, contentious, and occasionally bizarre place, but its politics are seldom dull. Because the state is geographically large and fragmented and ethnically and racially diverse, no single region or city is dominant.

The demographic changes in Florida during the past century have further complicated these regional divisions and led, not surprisingly, to a crisis about identity among its citizens. For much of its recent history Florida has been essentially two states—one that extends south from the Georgia border to Ocala and that has identified with the South and its social, political, and racial traditions, and another that extends north from Key West and Miami to just south of Ocala, with a heritage that typically has little connection to the South, that has historically had a diverse ethnic and racial population, and that has viewed the state as part of a national and international economy. A resident of Taylor County captured the sentiments of North Florida in 1993, when he commented, "We're a southern state and damn proud of it." But three hundred miles to the south, a resident of Dade County looked thoroughly bewildered when asked what it meant to be a southerner. Despite the claim of the Taylor County resident, only 35 percent of the state's population was actually born in Florida. Moreover, this population trend has moved steadily downward since 1970 as increasing numbers of people moved into Florida from other places in the United States and overseas. By 2000 fewer than half the state's residents had lived in Florida before 1970, and more Floridians had been born in New York than in any other state, excluding Florida.

The consequence has been that Floridians have little sense of their own identity, and few issues unite them as a people. The residents of Orlando, for example, believe that they have little in common with those who reside in Miami or Tallahassee. Tourism and the megatheme parks such as Disney World shape the worldview of those who live in Orlando. Hispanic residents of Miami similarly have little sense of North Florida and its residents and see them as potential enemies rather than as neighbors. Moreover, few Hispanics share much in common with each other. The large Cuban-American population dominates the region, but southeast Florida has many Hispanic people from Puerto Rico, as well as from such nations as the Dominican Republic, Nicaragua, Brazil, and Colombia.

The absence of a statewide identity occasionally reaches the trivial; for example, Floridians are free to purchase license plates that highlight their respective interests in panthers, manatees, public education, higher education, and veterans. Humorist Carl Hiassen has commented that Floridians are so divided that they cannot even agree about the design of their license plate.

Because an increasing number of whites feel beleaguered by diversity (of the state and the nation) and the growing political prominence of non-Anglo groups, and less in control of a society that these whites perceive as their own, sociologists have observed the resurgence of "white ethnicity." The development of this ethnic identity has been particularly true in Florida. In 1999, a barber in Gainesville, who is also a native of North Florida, reflected the concerns of white natives when he commented to one of the authors about Miami, "It is not a city in Florida, it is a foreign country." The tendency among Hispanic and black groups to vote as blocs on candidates and issues has intensified the concerns of whites. Although bloc voting is a historic pattern in the United States that was also common for most whites and white immigrant groups in the nineteenth and twentieth centuries, more recent generations of whites have tended to forget their own history in this regard and the reasons why minority groups often choose to coalesce as voting blocs.

As long as the state's economy remained strong and unemployment low, as was the case for much of the 1990s, ethnic and racial differences did not dominate the political and social discourse in Florida. However, the terrorist attacks on the World Trade Center and the Pentagon in September 2001 have had a significant economic impact and could change the racial and ethnic climate. For the time being, the Florida of the new century is not the economically and racially troubled California of 1996, when a group of angry white men took control of the ballot box and ended ethnic and racial preferences in their state. But that could change in an environment in which fear and economic uncertainty prevail.

Governor Jeb Bush sought to prevent a racial backlash in the state when he offered his "One Florida" initiative late in the fall of 2000. Although his plan avoided some of the worst features of Proposition 209 that Ward Connerly had championed in California, it also did away with affirmative action in university admissions and in state contracts. A series of sit-ins and marches that followed in Tallahassee and other parts of the state revealed the persistence of a racial divide in Florida, despite many advances since the days of segregation and Bush's promise to create greater opportunities for black citizens.[3]

Floridians would be naive at best if they thought this issue of race and diversity had been put to rest. Alienation and oppression frequently marked the history of twentieth-century Florida. A sudden or severe economic downturn would almost certainly propel the darker side of Florida's past to the fore and trigger a resurgence in the state's white ethnicity. Moreover, the demographic trends of the twenty-first century signal that racial and ethnic diversity will become increasingly prominent and assume a greater threat to whites in the process. How the state's white population responds to the gradual decline of its majority status will be a critical issue in the new millennium.

Looking into the Future

The demographic developments in Florida since the end of World War II have reshaped Florida and redefined state politics. Florida is a remarkably different state, politically, culturally, and economically, than the one that entered World War II. The demographic projections through 2025 suggest that Florida will continue to evolve significantly from the southern state that embraced the twentieth century and the Sunbelt state that entered the twenty-first century. Whether the transformation in the state's demographics will bring about the sort of fundamental changes that occurred in the second half of the twentieth century remains to be seen. But the graying of the state's population and its greater diversity suggest that change could once again be profound.

What, then, does the future hold for Florida? The safest prediction one can make about Florida is that its population growth will persist and that its political and social environment will continue to change as its population diversifies. In this book we briefly examine Florida's history in the nineteenth and twentieth centuries to provide a perspective on the changes since the mid-1800s and to place into context the changes that are projected to occur in the first twenty-five years of the new millennium.

We have avoided formulating a model of historical change in Florida; to do so would oversimplify and inevitably gloss over much of Florida's rich history and might exclude from consideration unique aspects of modern Florida that may well shape the Florida of tomorrow. However, we could not have written this book without using a general theoretical framework to help us divide the state's history into particular eras, sift important events from the vast rubble of the past, and select contemporary trends that will have the biggest influence on Florida's future. Our analysis has been guided by an image of Florida whose culture and politics are periodically stretched, and that sometimes hemorrhage, as a result of the influx of people with new values, lifestyles, and needs. Florida is definitely not a melting pot in the traditional sense of the term. Newcomers are not simply assimilated into Florida's established ways of thinking and behaving. Florida began the twentieth century rooted in the Confederacy and still angry about its place in the nation, but by the end of the century the Florida of the Old South had virtually disappeared under the changes wrought initially by railroad barons and land investors from the North, then by northeasterners and midwesterners who migrated after World War II, then by large numbers of retirees from the same regions, and simultaneously by immigrants from Cuba and Latin America.

We expect Florida will continue to experience dramatic change in the twenty-first century. First, demographers project that its senior population will increase by approximately 8 percent and comprise more than one in four residents. Second, the state's ethnic and racial diversity will become more complex as both the Hispanic and African-American populations increase in number, while the white population declines as a percentage of the total. Third, Florida's economy will diversify further, and South Florida will expand its influence throughout Latin America as a financial, economic, and cultural capital. With one foot firmly planted in Latin America, Florida will provide greater opportunities for people of color and immigrants from this region. Florida's government will not escape the effects of these significant changes. The state's southern politics will slowly fade away but not without some death throes. The state will reexamine its tax structure and perhaps reconfigure it as commerce moves increasingly to the Internet, but such reforms will inevitably raise questions about how to distribute the tax burden across different age groups, social classes, and economic sectors. Florida will impose further restrictions on urban sprawl to protect its water supply and its environment but not without conflict about where and how to draw the line between zones of urbanization and conservation. And the power of the governor will grow as the state responds to pressure from its large senior population and tries to balance the needs and demands of its white residents and its expanding ethnic and racial minorities, but charges of excessive executive influence will undoubtedly accompany this consolidation of power. In short, the future of Florida is potentially rife with controversy, a future perhaps already foretold by the disputed 2000 presidential election.

It is no wonder, then, that the nation will watch Florida closely in the twenty-first century. The demographic, economic, and political dynamics that will occur in Florida are likely to unfold in one way or another in the rest of the nation. Moreover, the leadership of the nation in the global economy and perhaps the creation of a new global world order is already commencing in Florida. How that transition occurs and what the changes in Florida portend for the United States are some of the developments that fascinate Americans about Florida.

chapter I

The Evolution of Florida to 1940

Florida as a Southern State

When Florida entered the twentieth century, its southern roots ran deep, nourished by history and by the adversity of the Civil War. The Deep South association grew out of mid-nineteenth-century migrations of people from Alabama and Georgia, both of which border Florida, and from South Carolina. These settlers gradually outnumbered other Floridians during the antebellum period and dominated political life in the state at the time of the Civil War. Most lived close to the Georgia and Alabama borders, where they re-created the southern culture of their former homes throughout the northern regions of Florida, from Ocala to Jacksonville and west to Pensacola. They also developed the plantation system, small farms, and timber and turpentine industries that reinforced economic and social ties with their Deep South neighbors.

The Civil War seared Florida's southern identity into the soul of its citizens and into the state's place in the nation for the next hundred years. The commitment of most white Floridians to the social and cultural values of the South and to slavery ensured their loyalty to the Confederacy, but civil conflict between secessionists and unionists persisted throughout the war years. Despite the suffering, turmoil, and eventual defeat during the Civil War, secessionists in Florida never doubted their decision, and in the aftermath of the bloody conflict they mourned "the Lost Cause" and "worshipped the Confederate dead and hated the Yankee living."[1] Memories of the Civil War and Reconstruction haunted these Floridians from 1876 through the first half of the twentieth century and often dominated the state's political culture.

Many remnants of the Civil War period remain visible today, especially in northern Florida. Memorials to Civil War veterans dot North Florida, and statues of Confederate leaders frequently dominate town squares. The state flag still retains some elements of the battle flag of the Confederacy, and the state song, "Old Folks at Home," opens with the lamentation "Way Down Upon the Suwannee River," in which an African American who migrated north yearns nostalgically for the ways of the South.

It is not surprising, then, that Florida's leaders, as with their counterparts in other southern states, did not accept the outcome of the Civil War willingly. At nearly every stage in the post–Civil War and Reconstruction process, Floridians resisted federal controls and took steps to preserve the social, political, and racial traditions of the past. Although the Florida Constitution of 1865 acknowledged the results of the Civil War by rescinding the ordinance of secession and abolishing slavery, it also prohibited blacks from voting and instituted a series of black codes to ensure white dominance and the regulation of black activities. An angry U.S. Congress controlled by radical Republicans denounced the actions of Florida and other southern states and passed the Military Reconstruction Acts on March 3, 1867, to oversee the readmission of the southern states under conditions that satisfied northern representatives.

The process of military Reconstruction traumatized Florida, and its effects would be felt for generations to come. Elements of the Union Army, including black soldiers, supervised the process for nearly nine years, until 1876. This era was a painful one for white Floridians, and they remained isolated from the national mainstream and mired in rural poverty for much of the late nineteenth and early twentieth centuries. Florida was an outcast among outcasts within the former Confederacy. In 1880, nine out of ten Floridians resided in rural areas, and the state's population was a mere 269,493, making it much smaller than Arkansas, the next smallest state in the South with 802,525 people (table 1). Key West was Florida's largest city with 9,800 residents, and only three cities in the entire state had more than 3,000 inhabitants.

The western frontier states attracted many more settlers than Florida, which Americans viewed as remote, swamplike, and inhospitable. Moreover, its lingering commitment to the antebellum period and its embrace of racial politics offered few incentives to migrants who were seeking a place to start over and build a new future for themselves.

Shortly after the collapse of military Reconstruction in 1876, native whites reasserted their control of state government and defied the 1868 constitution, which had implemented democratic procedures for voting and campaigning for political office. No one at the time realized that the state constitutional convention of 1885 would be providing the legal framework for state politics for the next eighty years, but that was the result. The constitution of 1885 grew out of the political and racial developments of the Civil War and Reconstruction era, and it represented a backlash against military Reconstruction and the democratic reforms of the 1868 constitution. The delegates to the constitutional convention of 1885 set about dismantling the powers that the 1868 constitution had granted to the governor, because this office had played a prominent role in the military Reconstruction of the state; the delegates also imposed a racial caste system that would ensure white supremacy. The new constitution prevented the governor from succeeding himself, established a cabinet system to weaken the executive branch, abolished the office of lieutenant governor, and stripped the governor of the substantial appointment powers vested in the office under the Reconstruction constitution as tools to reform the Confederate South. Additionally, the constitution segregated the schools and authorized a poll tax to limit black voting. The new constitution proved quite successful in reducing the authority of the governor and reasserting the dominance of northern Floridians and their political culture in state affairs.

The political legacy of Reconstruction continues to affect state government even in the twenty-first century. Florida has the most fragmented executive branch of any state in the nation, and the fragmentation is rooted in the post-Reconstruction era. Many states have officials, such as the attorney general or the commissioner of agriculture, for example, who are elected by statewide vote, but Florida is the only state in which these officials become part of the state cabinet and

Table 1. Population of Florida, the southeastern states, and the United States

Year	Florida	Alabama	Arkansas	Georgia	Kentucky	Louisiana	Mississippi
1880	29,493	1,262,505	802,525	1,542,180	1,648,690	939,946	1,131,597
1890	391,422	1,513,401	1,128,211	1,837,353	1,858,635	1,118,588	1,289,600
1900	528,542	1,828,697	1,311,564	2,216,331	2,147,174	1,381,625	1,551,270
1910	752,619	2,138,093	1,574,449	2,609,121	2,289,905	1,656,388	1,797,114
1920	968,470	2,348,174	1,752,204	2,895,832	2,416,630	1,798,509	1,790,618
1930	1,468,211	2,646,248	1,854,482	2,908,506	2,614,589	2,101,593	2,009,821
1940	1,897,414	2,832,961	1,949,387	3,123,723	2,845,627	2,363,880	2,183,796
1950	2,771,305	3,061,743	1,909,511	3,444,578	2,944,806	2,683,516	2,178,914
1960	4,951,560	3,266,740	1,786,272	3,943,116	3,038,156	3,257,022	2,178,141
1970	6,789,443	3,444,165	1,923,295	4,589,575	3,218,706	3,641,306	2,216,912
1980	9,746,324	3,893,888	2,286,435	5,463,105	3,660,777	4,205,900	2,520,638
1990	12,937,926	4,040,587	2,350,725	6,478,216	3,685,296	4,219,973	2,573,216
2000	15,982,378	4,447,100	2,673,400	8,186,453	4,041,769	4,468,976	2,844,658

Year	North Carolina	South Carolina	Tennessee	Virginia	West Virginia	U.S.
1880	1,399,750	995,577	1,542,359	1,512,565	618,457	50,189,209
1890	1,617,949	1,151,149	1,767,518	1,655,980	762,794	62,979,766
1900	1,893,810	1,340,316	2,020,616	1,854,184	958,800	76,212,168
1910	2,206,287	1,515,400	2,184,789	2,061,612	1,221,119	92,228,496
1920	2,559,123	1,683,724	2,337,885	2,309,187	1,463,701	106,021,537
1930	3,170,276	1,738,765	2,616,556	2,421,851	1,729,205	123,202,624
1940	3,571,623	1,899,804	2,915,841	2,677,773	1,091,974	132,164,569
1950	4,061,929	2,117,027	3,291,718	3,318,680	2,005,552	151,325,798
1960	4,556,155	2,382,594	3,567,089	3,966,949	1,860,421	179,323,175
1970	5,082,059	2,590,516	3,923,687	4,648,494	1,744,237	203,184,772
1980	5,881,766	3,121,820	4,591,120	5,346,818	1,949,644	226,542,199
1990	6,628,637	3,486,703	4,877,185	6,187,358	1,793,477	248,709,873
2000	8,049,313	4,012,012	5,689,283	7,078,515	1,808,344	281,421,906

Sources: U.S. Department of Commerce, Bureau of the Census, *Census of the Population 1960*, vol. 1, pt. 2; *1970 Census of the Population and General Population Characteristics*, Advance report for each state.

have an equal vote with the governor on a host of executive decisions. While recent constitutional amendments have eliminated some cabinet posts and strengthened the hand of the governor, the political distrust of central authority that originated in the Civil War and the Reconstruction era lingers in Florida in ways that no one in 1885 would have imagined and that few in the twenty-first century understand.

Having retaken control of their state, Florida's political leaders and citizens anxiously searched for ways to expand the economy, which had only slightly recovered from the devastation of the Civil War and Reconstruction. When the promise of a "New South" appeared at the end of the nineteenth century, with a pledge by its advocates to modernize and industrialize the region and bring it into the national mainstream, Floridians, especially those in its cities, eagerly embraced this New South movement in the hope that it would enable the state to become part of the national economic mainstream and spur economic development. Floridians actively courted the land developer Hamilton Disston, the railroad magnates Henry Flagler, William D. Chipley, and Henry B. Plant, and other wealthy investors, often throwing acres of free land at them and negotiating deals, frequently out of a sense of desperation, that would come back to haunt the state. The chummy and corrupting relationship between political leaders and businessmen was never more obvious than when Governor William Sherman Jennings (1901–5) signed a special divorce bill in 1901 so that Flagler could divorce his second wife, who was in a mental institution, and remarry. The succumbing of the legislature and governor to Flagler's economic influence in this manner was such a public embarrassment that legislators quickly rescinded the law in the next session in 1903, but Flagler had what he wanted, as had others before him.[2] Despite the efforts of Floridians to embrace the economic promise of the New South and despite the important contributions of industrial magnates to the state's development, the New South generally stayed well north of Florida, and economic expansion went elsewhere. Nevertheless, railroad construction had made much of the state accessible for the first time and set the stage for Florida's development in the twentieth century.

At about the same time Democrats also reestablished a caste system, at first informally and then through law, that permeated the entire state, denying its large African-American population (approximately 43 percent of residents in 1890) the rights guaranteed by the U.S. Constitution and the amendments adopted during Reconstruction. Despite opposition from the state Republican Party and resistance from black residents, who vigorously defended their right to the franchise, the Jim Crow system hardened into law in the 1890s and imposed a second-class status on African Americans until well into the second half of the twentieth century. White Floridians, as with other southerners, became entrapped culturally, economically, and politically by this self-imposed racist system. It thwarted Florida's ability to take full advantage of its human resources and deterred its integration into the national fabric.

A major development of this era that would have long-term consequences was the geographic segregation of African Americans in Florida. Many cities in the state in the late nineteenth century restricted black residential areas to the other side of the railroad tracks or to the outskirts of town. Cities on both the east and west coasts of Florida zoned housing for African Americans along a narrow strip of land that paralleled the railroad tracks. As a consequence, black communities in the state tended to be highly concentrated and distributed in a linear fashion running from north to south. These zoning patterns help explain why the predominantly black congressional and legislative districts of the late twentieth and early twenty-first centuries have taken such peculiar forms.

Florida's two-primary system constitutes another remnant of this era. The two-primary system, white primary, and poll tax assured white Floridians in the early twentieth century that a black candidate could not get elected. In a one-primary system in which the top vote-getter automatically becomes the party's nominee, a black candidate could win if two white candidates split the white vote and if black voters concentrate their votes. But the two-primary system made it impossible for a black candidate to win because it required the two leading candidates to meet in a runoff election, and whites could then vote en masse for the white candidate. The Democratic white primary subsequently restricted voting to whites only, and the poll tax of two dollars prevented poor blacks from voting in the general election.

In 1910 more than half the citizens of Florida of both races lived in small towns and in rural areas. Jacksonville, a center for the railroad and timber industries, remained the state's largest city with nearly 58,000 people. But the state's other cities were remarkably small: Miami's population stood at 5,400, St. Petersburg's at 4,100 people.

The racial politics of this era also impeded efforts by women to obtain the vote and to become involved in the political and economic life of the state. Women led the fight for temperance in Florida, and most of these women then served as leaders in the campaign for the suffrage. White males in the state, however, had no interest in allowing women with modern ideas to reshape their state and to redefine the place of women in society. White men also worried that black women would disrupt their political dominance if allowed to vote. Florida refused to support the submission to voters of the Nineteenth Amendment to the U.S. Constitution, and Floridians did not ratify women's suffrage until it did so—symbolically—in 1969 on the fiftieth anniversary of the establishment of the Florida League of Women Voters. Much like those in other southern states, white men in Florida placed white women on a pedestal as paragons of white superiority and genteel behavior. They were not to be sullied by such common and manly pursuits as politics. The gendered and racial construction of Florida society confined women as tightly as the corsets they wore during this era. Nevertheless, as soon as the Nineteenth Amendment was adopted nationally in 1921, women in Florida went to the polls to vote, and two ran for state office—Katherine Tippetts of St. Petersburg and Myrtice Vera McCaskill of Taylor County. Although both were defeated, it quickly became clear that women in Florida would not sit passively and let men decide their future and the political direction of the state. In 1928 Edna Giles Fuller of Orange County became the first woman elected to office in Florida as a member of the state House of Representatives. The leading voices for women's issues during this period were May Mann Jennings, wife of former governor William S. Jennings, and members of the Florida State League of Women Voters. Jennings and the league championed such reforms as child labor laws and the rights of women to serve on juries (not granted until 1949) and to manage their own property (not granted until 1944). They also launched reforms in the environmental area and in workplace and consumer product safety.³ Despite their efforts, however, the southern and racial culture of the state made it exceedingly difficult for women to be taken seriously before 1945.

Boom and Bust, 1920–1940

The 1920s offered hope to Floridians that their dreams of economic growth and prosperity would finally be secured, and then it left those hopes dashed—even before the Great Depression devastated the rest of the country. The roller coaster ride that Florida's economy experienced in the 1920s was so severe that the state seemed to drift through the 1930s, virtually paralyzed by what had happened.

The economic development and population growth that Florida had long sought occurred in astonishing fashion as the twenties began. The nation's economic expansion and the Wall Street boom that began in 1920 provided Americans with income to spend, and investors looked to an untapped Florida to make their next fortune.

Florida was thus "discovered," and growth was so dramatic that Florida's political leaders served as little more than cheerleaders for the boom. Towns sprang up along the coast and in areas that were formerly little more than swamps. Writers and journalists fanned the speculation mentality in Florida. A northern journalist captured the extent of the exaggeration about migration into the state when he wrote, "Was there ever anything like the migration into Florida? From the time the Hebrews went into Egypt, or since the hegira of Mohammed the prophet, what can compare to this evacuation? . . . Entire populations are moving away bodily. The personal columns of our local press are unable to chronicle the daily departures."⁴

People from the North and Midwest rushed into South Florida to profit from the development along the gold coast from West Palm Beach to Miami. The state's population increased by 500,000 people, from 968,470 in 1920 to 1,468,211 in 1930. Miami quadrupled in size, from 29,571 to 110,637, and closed the gap behind the state's largest city, Jacksonville, which had 129,549 residents. Tampa and St. Petersburg also boomed, and their combined population soared to 141,586.

Property on Miami Beach, which Carl Fisher, a developer, had offered to give away in 1915 to attract residents, went for $25,000 an acre and more in the early 1920s. Will Rogers commented, "Had there been no Carl Fisher, Florida would be known as the Turpentine State." Fisher marketed Miami Beach in the late teens by using such gimmicks as real estate advertisements that featured photographs of bathing beauties at the beach. He told employees, "We'll get the prettiest girls we can find and put them into the . . . tightest bathing suits and no stockings or swim shoes either. We'll have the pictures taken and send them all over the country."[5] Miami Beach became the hot spot for land purchases, and the *Miami News* made large sums of money, not through increased readership but by advertising land for sale. Northern speculators read the ads and threw money at new property offered for sale. A large, somewhat unscrupulous, sales force quickly appeared to capitalize on investors' fascination with Florida real estate. Referred to as "Binder Boys," these hucksters bought lots for 10 percent down (a binder that held the property for thirty days) and then sold the binders to other speculators. It was a shaky scheme, with investors confident that their purchase of Florida's land would bring them a quick fortune.[6]

Cities and counties also threw caution to the wind as each tried to wrest the golden goose from Miami and West Palm Beach. Most ended up deeply in debt or bankrupt, constructing road and tourist facilities in the belief that if you built them, the investors and residents would come. In many cases they did not. The state's political leaders fueled the speculative activities of local government in 1924, adopting a $500 tax exemption on household goods and personal effects for heads of families residing in the state. This tax inducement to those who relocated to Florida undermined local revenues, making it difficult for communities to provide the infrastructure to meet the demands of rapid growth. It also made local governments more vulnerable to a sudden economic decline.

When Florida's economy suddenly lurched downward in 1925, Floridians were ill equipped and ill prepared to do anything about it. Buoyed by the new wealth, state leaders had done little to regulate speculators or to restrain the massive debt that towns and counties incurred in an effort to attract investors. By 1926 Florida had sunk into a depression, three years before the rest of the nation, and remained mired there for fourteen long years.

Florida became a metaphor for the boom-and-bust years of the 1920s, and no other state experienced the highs and lows more thoroughly. Signs of decline appeared in 1925, when national newspapers and magazines warned investors about land fraud in Florida. The Binder Boys suddenly found themselves without an audience and, worse yet, without investors. By July 1926 the *Nation* reported, "The world's greatest poker game, played with building lots instead of chips, is over. And the players are now . . . paying up."[7] In the fall a severe hurricane revealed Florida's environmental vulnerability, completely swamping Miami Beach and causing 392 deaths. After an even more devastating storm in 1928 left an estimated 2,000 Floridians dead, investors withdrew en masse. A fruit fly infestation that destroyed 72 percent of the state's citrus trees and the onset of the national depression in 1929 were the coups de grâce. Per capita spending in Florida declined by 58 percent in the five years from 1926 to 1931. State and local tax collections fell from $62.23 to $47.84 per capita, and state banking reserves virtually collapsed, from $593 million to a mere $60 million. Nearly 220 banks in the state failed during this period. By the time the stock market died in the fall of 1929, Florida had already been mired in three years of depression so severe that some counties had to forfeit on their bonds, close their schools, and in a few cases declare bankruptcy. Key West was among the hardest hit, with the town bankrupt and more than 80 percent of the residents on relief.

The financial collapse of the 1920s paralyzed political leaders and left the state in a poor position to address the crisis. Governor Doyle Carlton (1929–33) attempted to counter the political ineptitude by urging legislators to raise taxes to reduce a state deficit of $2.5 million and to assist counties in paying off their bonds. He also sought a gasoline tax to pay for roads and to keep schools open. But the governor's tax plan encountered stiff opposition from those representatives whose counties had small debts, most of them in North Florida, and who felt they were being forced to pay for the sins of those who had risked all during the boom years. The conflict and distrust between North and

South Florida that would dominate state politics from 1945 to 1968 took form during the 1920s, with many in North Florida viewing the profligate South Florida as fully deserving of what had happened to it. No North Florida politician was willing to support financial plans to bail the region out. Fistfights broke out on the floor of the legislature as members angrily debated the governor's relief proposals and as the economy continued to worsen. North Floridians suffered as well, but most were small farmers who were self-supporting, never had much cash, and could at least feed themselves. At one point a totally exasperated Carlton pleaded with legislators, "If the program that has been offered does not meet with your liking, then for God's sake provide one that does."[8]

Carlton's successors, David Sholtz (1933–37) and Fred Cone (1937–41), refused to follow Carlton's controversial lead and instead urged economy in government. Eight candidates sought the governorship in 1932, fourteen in 1936, and eleven in 1940, leading political pundits to suggest that a man had to run for governor in order to make a living in Florida during the depression. Both Sholtz and Cone blamed Florida's problems on irresponsible leadership and called for a return to fiscal restraint, balanced budgets, and sound business principles. Their proposals offered Floridians essentially no relief. In 1932, with nearly 30 percent of the population unemployed and state governors offering little hope or vision, voters embraced the Democratic candidate for president, Franklin D. Roosevelt, with a sense of desperation. The New York governor received 75 percent of the votes cast in Florida, while the incumbent president Herbert Hoover, who had carried the state in the 1928 election, received fewer than 25 percent of the ballots. Floridians anxiously awaited Roosevelt's inauguration in March 1933 and the promise of much needed federal relief. Roosevelt's New Deal programs kept Florida solvent during the 1930s. The president's buoyant attitude and his ties to the South through his winter home in Warm Springs, Georgia, gave hope and recognition to the region and to Florida in particular. Portraits of Roosevelt appeared alongside pictures of Jesus in many Florida homes. Most saw Roosevelt as the modern savior of the state. A desperate Florida turned the administration of Key West over to the Federal Emergency Relief Administration, and residents were put to work cleaning streets, renovating homes and city facilities, and improving beaches. The Agricultural Adjustment Act of 1933 provided crucial assistance for financially troubled farmers and grove owners.

The federal government also offered substantial programmatic and financial assistance to Florida for flood control projects and for a planned Florida intracoastal waterway. Following the devastating 1928 hurricane, which dropped a wall of water on the communities in the southeast, flooded farmlands throughout the Lake Okeechobee area, and killed 2,000 people, the Hoover and Roosevelt administrations provided nearly $19 million to build the Hoover Dike and drainage canal around the lake. During this same period hopes revived for a waterway that would extend from Jacksonville to Tampa Bay, opening a way for shipping to move speedily from the Atlantic into the Gulf of Mexico. Most north Floridians, especially those along the canal, viewed the project as a much needed economic boost for the region. But South Floridians worried about the effects of the dredging on their supply of fresh water and of the new canal on Tampa's expanding port facilities. The state's influential railroad leaders, who saw the canal as a serious threat to their economic future, joined forces with those in opposition.

But despite warnings from the U.S. Geological Survey that "there appears to be no reasonable doubt that serious adverse affects will be produced upon the important underground water supplies of the Ocala limestone," Roosevelt decided to proceed with funding for the project. Pressure from Florida's congressional leaders and from those of other states along the Gulf Coast seemed to have sealed the matter. But the project would bedevil Roosevelt and more especially politicians at the state and local levels who supported it. In a move that came to be symbolic of the controversy that ultimately surrounded the project, Roosevelt launched the excavation from his family home in Hyde Park, New York. Hundreds gathered in Ocala for the event. Then Roosevelt prematurely pressed a telegraph button that triggered an explosion from New York while Democratic senator Duncan Fletcher of Florida was in the middle of his speech, sending people scurrying for cover and leaving them covered with dirt, rumpled, and more than a bit stunned.[9]

It marked a tumultuous beginning for what would always be a contentious project—the Cross-Florida Barge Canal.

Frantic for economic assistance and for any project that would ease the suffering of residents, Governor Sholtz cast the fate of his administration with the New Deal and his personal relationship with Roosevelt. The president provided Florida with a safety net that halted the downward spiral of state and personal finances. At the same time rumors—never proved—circulated that Sholtz had assured his financial future by secretly receiving money from Florida's parimutuel interests. But ordinary Floridians continued to suffer greatly during the 1930s. The New Deal provided some crucial relief, and the leadership and the economy began to stabilize in 1936 as tourists began reappearing. New hotels sprang up in Miami and Miami Beach, but the state had no significant signs of prosperity as late as 1939.

By the end of the economically troubled decade of the 1930s, Florida's population had expanded to nearly 1.9 million, but the growth rate had slowed measurably during the depression years, and much of the state remained sparsely settled. Orlando, for example, had only 27,000 people, and much of the southwest coast of Florida stood relatively undeveloped. The population of Fort Myers was only 9,000, and Naples was little more than a village. The draining of the Everglades strengthened commercial agriculture and made it more profitable. Slowly, tourism began to lift the state out of the depression in the late 1930s. Agriculture also began to revive, aided by an oppressive migrant labor policy—farmers and law enforcement officials cooperated with one another to provide a much needed pool of cheap labor that facilitated agricultural productivity.

Despite the growth of the 1920s and 1930s and the increasing urbanization of the state's population, Florida looked remarkably similar to the Florida of 1900. The Democratic Party still had a hammerlock on state politics, and representatives from North Florida controlled both houses of the legislature. Republicans had no representation in the legislature until the election of Alex Akerman of Orlando in 1945. Black Floridians continued to suffer under the oppression of segregation, and the depression had taken a devastating toll on black family life. Young black men fled to the North during the 1930s, searching for freedom and opportunity, and most never returned. Only limited federal assistance, passed through the hands of white farmers and citrus owners, found its way into the pockets of black farmers and black tenants. These meager funds, however, were often the difference between destitution and economic survival. The state still relied on agriculture, railroads, and the lumber business for most of its economic vitality, much as it had in the first decade of the twentieth century, although tourism had reemerged in the late 1930s as a potentially more lucrative source of wealth than any of these other activities. Florida's political and economic leaders continued to seek growth under nearly any conditions, especially after more than a decade of depression. Their appeals to business interests in other states were ignored, however, as few saw Florida as a land of opportunity.

The state's population gradually shifted during this era with the growth of the cities of Miami and Tampa, so that most Floridians lived in urban areas by the 1930s, but residents still viewed themselves as small-town folks. And they continued to hold tightly to conservative political, religious, and social values. The depression had curtailed their optimism about the future and their confidence in the state's political leadership, but their faith in God and in fundamental Christian values had not changed.

In some significant ways, however, the 1920s and 1930s presaged the transformation that would occur in subsequent decades. Florida's increasing reliance on the federal government constituted one such development. Following the onset of the depression in the state in 1926 and the devastating hurricane of 1928, Florida sought federal assistance to ease the crisis and to protect Floridians from severe flooding. In the 1930s New Deal programs offered federal largesse through relief for farmers, social security for the unemployed, and flood relief projects for residents in South Florida.

A second major development was the support of Florida voters for Hoover in the election of 1928. Their defection to the "Party of Lincoln" gave early evidence that voters would abandon the national Democratic Party if it and its candidates did not represent their values. Al Smith, the Democratic candidate for president in 1928, epitomized all the values that Floridians opposed. He was an ethnic American and a member of the big-city political machine Tammany Hall, supported an end to Prohibition, and, worst of all, was Roman Catholic.

Thus despite the collapse of the short-lived economic boom of the 1920s and the onset of a stifling fourteen-year depression, subtle changes had begun that would reshape the state in the postwar years. But none of these developments would influence Florida and its future as significantly as the coming war. Indeed, World War II would finally end the state's long economic drought and launch an era of dramatic growth that would change Florida forever.

In an effort to persuade Americans to settle Florida, land drawings were held in the late nineteenth century. The drawings helped, but Florida's intense summer climate and the abundant pests proved too much even for those seeking cheap land and a chance to start over. It took a hardy soul to brave Florida's summer environment prior to World War II.

Six Seminole women gather in native dress with two children. Despite generally peaceful relations between Seminoles and early Florida settlers, conditions changed as more and more people moved into the state. Seminole lands were seized, and nearly all the natives were sent with the Cherokees to Oklahoma. Today, the Seminoles are few in number, but they have enjoyed something of an economic renaissance with the opening of gambling casinos on their land.

A grocery store in nineteenth-century Florida where white and black citizens all gathered to shop and to socialize. Social interaction between the races was brief and cordial. Racial lines had been drawn, though, making clear the proper place of whites and blacks, but often these divisions were less obvious in small towns where families of both races knew each other.

Governors William Jennings and Napoleon Broward in the Everglades, where drainage to control flooding and to provide land for the ever-expanding population of southeast Florida was going forward.

Dredging the Everglades proved to be an environmental disaster, but nearly every-one saw it as progress. The belief in people's ability to alter the environment to suit their needs and purposes was widely accepted. In this photograph, dredging gets under way aboard a dredging ship.

Governor Sidney J. Catts in his inaugural parade in January 1917. Elected as the can-didate of the Prohibition Party, he was the only person to be elected governor in the twentieth century under the banner of a third party. An electrifying personality, he drove his Ford throughout much of the state to take his candidacy to the people.

A farmer in the cane fields of south Florida gathers in sugarcane and begins the process of pressing it into syrup. The picture captures the primitive conditions and isolation of those involved in this farming industry.

Native Floridians enjoyed the state's natural beauty. Once the intensity of summer had passed, residents often had picnics on the rivers and at the springs and ocean in the 1910s and 1920s. In this photograph, residents of the Peace River area enjoy an afternoon picnic.

Above: The Great Depression arrived in Florida in 1926, three years before the rest of the nation. Its devastating effects touched the lives of nearly every man, woman, and child in the state. This man sits on the bumper of his house-car with nothing to do and nowhere to go.

Left: The Everglades were viewed as a rich resource for state development, and some believed that oil existed in the region. Fortunately, it was not the case, and the Everglades was spared this calamity.

Like vegetable crops, the citrus industry found Florida's soil and sun appealing. By the late nineteenth century, many whites had developed citrus groves in central and south Florida. The industry became highly profitable as demand grew in the North. Cheap black labor, as evidenced in this photograph, helped to keep costs low.

For much of its history, Florida has been a place where vegetable crops have been grown. Its long growing season provided opportunity for two crops. The harvesting of these crops, such as the tomatoes shown in the picture, was often the work of blacks from the local community. This was demanding work at very low wages.

Florida was rich in phosphate, and the mining of it dominated the economy in the late nineteenth and early twentieth centuries. The process was extremely destructive to the environment, however, often leaving limestone caverns and polluted water runoff.

chapter 2

World War II and
the Modernization of Florida

Between 1940 and 1970 the Old South and the New South collided in Florida, causing tremendous social upheaval and fundamentally changing the state. From the perspective of the twenty-first century Florida's modern form may have seemed inevitable, but it came slowly, haltingly, violently, and often without clear direction. Driven in large part by the massive influx of new residents, Florida's modernization and rise to national prominence in the late twentieth century occurred in fits and starts because of several factors. Foremost among them was a deeply rooted culture of the Old South that was not easily changed by population growth and that was bolstered by the political dominance of rural North Florida. Because newcomers to Florida were slow to pursue political and social change as they adjusted to life in their adopted state, North Floridians were able to gather their forces and fend off change for decades. Without the intervention of the federal government and the federal courts, Florida's modernization would have been even more fractious and would have taken longer to develop, and it may well have taken an entirely different form.

Although Florida's economic development was probably inevitable, given its semitropical climate, its lush environment, its lengthy and sublime coastline, and its beautiful beaches, the state's economic resurgence did not commence until the 1940s with the infusion of massive federal expenditures and the migration of more than 2.1 million men and women into the state for military training. The news of the attack on Pearl Harbor in December 1941 unified the nation as nothing ever had and brought Florida fully into the national mainstream. Other than perhaps the Great Depression, no event was more momentous for the nation in the twentieth century, and certainly none was more consequential for Florida. The war not only unified the nation, it also ended the suffocating economic crisis that had paralyzed the country and the state and began the modern development of Florida.

Florida's development in the second half of the twentieth century would be unprecedented, and population demographics reveal just how astonishing it was. In the growth of its population alone, Florida became a startlingly different place in a mere sixty years. As the statistics in table 2 make clear, Florida's population boom began during World War II, and the Florida that most of us know today is, in large measure, a post–World War II development.

As historian Gary Mormino has observed, after the United States declared war on December 8, 1941, "Florida became a garrison state, armed and trained [men and women] for every conceivable military function."[1] The federal government opened major military bases throughout the state to meet the demands of its navy and air force in particular, and tens of thousands of laborers poured into the state to work at air bases and in shipyards in Jacksonville, Panama City, Pensacola, and Tampa. Miami Beach alone saw 70,000 hotel rooms taken over by the Army Air Force in 1942. The arrival of service personnel, workers, and their families quickly generated full employment and led to the dramatic expansion of Florida's cities from Miami to Jacksonville and west to Pensacola. Camp Blanding, a remote outpost near Jacksonville, felt the consequences of the buildup more than most places, becoming the state's fourth largest city during the war, with 55,000 army personnel. The base spread over 180,000 acres and had 125 miles of paved road provided by the federal government. At Camp Gordon Johnston in Carrabelle, thousands of men trained for sea invasions that would subsequently be conducted in North Africa, Sicily, Normandy, and Okinawa. Naval and air bases sprang up from Tampa to Jacksonville and Pensacola. Florida's coastline became a natural area for training navy personnel. Its extended shipping lanes, however, were also exceedingly vulnerable to attacks by enemy submarines.

Not only did the federal government build bases and train men and women on them; it also constructed modern transportation facilities to

Table 2. Florida's population growth in the twentieth century

Year	Population	Growth in decade
1900	528,542	137,120
1910	752,619	224,077
1920	968,470	215,851
1930	1,468,211	499,741
1940	1,897,414	429,203
1950	2,771,305	873,891
1960	4,951,560	2,180,255
1970	6,789,443	1,839,858
1980	9,746,324	2,954,906
1990	12,937,926	3,191,602
2000	15,982,378	3,044,452

move troops and supplies. In the process soldiers and their families generated an enormous demand for goods and services. The military construction projects were a boon to Florida's communities, stimulating dramatic economic expansion and development unlike that seen since the early 1920s. Floridians responded by developing new products to aid the military, but none of the others had quite the effect on the state's postwar economy as the development of frozen concentrated orange juice.

The war also created new opportunities for the half-million black residents of Florida, and the war propaganda gave them hope that racial change would be forthcoming. Significantly, it would be the last war in which Americans would serve in segregated units. In contrast to the eighteen months of U.S. participation in World War I, the four years of World War II and the concomitant social and geographic dislocation mobilized the black community behind racial reform in ways the country had not yet seen. Leaders of the National Association for the Advancement of Colored People seized the political initiative at the beginning of the conflict and called on black Americans and whites to embrace the "Double V" campaign: victory against racism overseas and against racism at home. The U.S. military's propaganda assault on Germany and Japan placed the nation and its state governments in an uncomfortable position as officials attempted to mobilize the public behind the war effort and against its racist foes while simultaneously trying to maintain segregation in the South. This dilemma was apparent not only to blacks but became increasingly so to whites, many of whom were displeased with the nation's racial policies. In Florida, Herbert Krensky, traveling by train from Miami to Jacksonville during the war, watched in stunned silence as a platoon of German prisoners of war boarded the train, while the conductor turned away black servicemen, one of whom was on crutches. Krensky recalled that the conductor told the servicemen that "since there were no colored coaches . . . they would have to ride in the baggage car."[2] Despite the general resistance to racial change throughout the United States and among southern representatives in Congress, black Americans discovered more and more allies, especially on the federal bench and in the federal government, who shared Krensky's abhorrence of the treatment of black veterans and black citizens.

World War II also spurred the mobility of Americans, forcing many to leave home for the first time and acquainting them with Americans from all sorts of ethnic and racial backgrounds and with the various regions of the country. The war uprooted an estimated 31 million Americans, approximately 25 percent of the population. Hundreds of thousands of people came to Florida for the first time, and many liked what they saw. A young Virginian, Dan Moody, wrote home to his parents after arriving in Miami Beach on January 29, 1944, and being housed in the Hotel Blackstone, "Mother, this is the most beautiful place that I have ever seen. . . . I really think when the war is over, I'll move down here."[3] He would not be alone.

Despite fears generated by the war, Floridians embraced many of the changes that occurred, as well as scientific advances that promised to make Florida more accessible. The introduction of effective mosquito control through the use of DDT in the last year of the war made the state more appealing to newcomers and awakened them to the state's enormous potential. The nearly five months of summer had made Florida almost intolerable to all but the hardiest of souls. But pest control suddenly made much of the year bearable, and the gradual introduction of air-conditioning during the war and postwar years overcame the oppressive heat and humidity of summer. The rest of the year had always been appealing to the rich from the North; with new roads and improved living conditions, Florida now became accessible to the middle class.

During the 1940s nearly 900,000 people moved to Florida permanently, despite the dislocation and lack of permanence created by the war effort in the first half of the decade. Florida had been discovered once again, but unlike the 1920s, this time its discovery would not be short lived. Most new arrivals settled in South Florida, particularly in the southeastern and southwestern corners of the state. Those who settled on the southeast coast generally came from the northeastern region of the United States, while those who settled along the southwest coast came principally from the Midwest, leading one pundit to observe that as one goes south in Florida, one actually moves north. And this was certainly true in terms of the state's culture. By the 1950s these two southern regions of Florida had a majority of the state's inhabitants, but they had, by no means, a majority of the state's legislative representatives.

The War and Economic Development

Led by Governor Spessard Holland (1941–45), Florida worked closely with the Roosevelt administration and the War Department to secure federal funds for Florida, both to defend its coastline and troop trains and to help provide an economic and transportation infrastructure that would secure the state's future. Although criticizing a bloated federal government and condemning its interference in state and local affairs became politically fashionable in the 1980s and 1990s, Florida would not have prospered as quickly or as successfully without federal investment during the war and postwar years. The federal government provided the financial capital as well as the human capital that facilitated Florida's postwar growth. A modern military-industrial economy took hold. The actions and the policies of the federal government shaped Florida's modernization in the twentieth century, and in most cases these policies benefited the state's citizens.

With the war and the federal government providing a much needed economic boost, Florida's leaders sought to capitalize on the changes taking place by marketing the state to the nation. Holland's successor,

Millard Caldwell (1945–49), encouraged tourists and potential residents to come to Florida by dramatically expanding the activities of the Florida Department of Commerce. Caldwell sought to offset what many feared—the possibility of a severe postwar economic recession and another collapse of the Florida Dream of beautiful beaches, sun and youth, and personal renewal. The marketing strategy took various forms, but fundamentally it sought to sell the nation on an image of Florida as a place of opportunity, freedom, youth, and beauty. Commerce Department employees seemed to take a devilish pleasure in sending photographs of beautiful young women, scantily clad in bathing suits and lounging near an outdoor pool or by the ocean, to northern newspapers in the dead of winter. Whether it was the advertisements or better roads and better automobiles, snowbirds from as far north as Canada came in search of the fountain of youth and warmth. The beauty and warmth of the place revitalized visitors who labored through the harsh winter months back home. After spending a few winters in Florida, many decided not to return home. Florida experienced no postwar recession as a consequence, much to the relief of state leaders and residents, and the Florida Dream no longer seemed such a distant possibility to many middle-class Americans.

Florida's growth exploded in the postwar period from 1945 to 1960. Population growth averaged 558 people per day during this fifteen-year period, with more than 700 per day arriving in several years of the 1950s. More people moved to Florida in this period than had lived in the state in all the years before 1920. The pressure of this growth, alongside the massive influx of middle-class tourists who had suddenly discovered Florida, created a new day-to-day crisis in the state. Compounding these problems, tourists occasionally collided with the cows that freely roamed the highways and byways, destroying their cars and in some cases killing the tourists. Then the farmers sued the tourists and new residents for the deaths of their cows. Florida was unprepared and ill equipped to handle the population and tourist explosion. New residents complained about poor schools, insufficient housing, and inadequate police and fire services, and tourists griped about the number and quality of hotel and motel facilities. But none of these problems slowed the human wave descending on the state.

Despite the massive migration, Florida's sales pitch to prospective businesses and residents remained essentially the same from 1945 to 1980 and differed only slightly from that used before the war. Emphasizing low taxes, a healthy environment, inexpensive land, and a pro-business political climate, state agencies, led by the governor's office, appealed to potential investors throughout the nation but especially to those east of the Mississippi. The war years, a healthy national economy, tourism, good roads, and eventually air-conditioning were instrumental in making the appeal successful. Governor Caldwell and his successors undertook a series of trips to the Northeast and Midwest in an effort to recruit new business and commerce. These trips gradually expanded in subsequent gubernatorial administrations to include Western Europe, Latin America, and the Far East as Florida attempted to internationalize its economy and its tourism. The state rapidly modernized its roads in the postwar period, again aided by the federal government, to accommodate increasing automobile traffic and economic development. Caldwell's successor, Fuller Warren (1949–53), finally pushed through a fence law to keep the cattle from killing residents and tourists.[4] By accepting Warren's fence proposal, Florida had crossed the Rubicon, acknowledging that the health and well-being of tourists meant more to the state's future than its agricultural interests.

Racial Developments in the War and Postwar Years

While Florida and its state political leaders basked in the war and postwar economic boom, they also kept a wary eye on racial developments, determined to maintain continuity in race relations from the prewar era. The social and political upheaval threatened by Florida's dramatic population growth and the demands of black citizens had not escaped the attention of legislative leaders from North Florida. Efforts to reapportion the legislature in recognition of the growth of South Florida suddenly became more politically volatile, but few such proposals ever made it to the floor of either chamber in Tallahassee in the 1940s and 1950s. North Florida representatives beat back all such efforts, determined to protect their political hegemony as well as the interests and values of their region against those of the new residents of South Florida.

At the same time, efforts by Governor Caldwell and his successors to streamline state government through reorganization met with consistent legislative opposition. Rural legislators were reluctant to allow even a governor like Caldwell, who shared their political and social convictions, to strengthen the hand of the governor's office at the expense of the legislature. These same legislators were well aware that, because the urban south held a majority of votes in statewide elections, North Florida was going to lose control of the governor's office. The last thing the North Florida legislators wanted was a stronger governor's office occupied by someone elected by South Florida.

In the 1940s and 1950s, as black civil rights leaders and the federal courts began to challenge the South's segregation laws, the disparity in salaries of black and of white teachers, and the white primary laws, the state's governors, led by Caldwell and Warren, did what the federal courts required of Florida, but they stonewalled federal intent at every turn. Caldwell, for example, persuaded the legislature to adopt the Minimum Foundations Program for the public schools. Such legislation was common in the South in the postwar period and had two essential purposes. One was to strengthen the educational system in the region by giving school systems more money so that southern states could become more competitive in recruiting and developing new businesses and so that the native population would have more economic opportunities. The other aim, however, was to upgrade black schools in the region so that the federal courts could not rule that public education in the South was unequal.[5] In the 1940s and early 1950s federal judges had signaled their dissatisfaction with the region's funding of black schools, which often stood in desperate need of repair, and black teacher salaries, which were typically one-fourth of those for white teachers. Avoiding the intervention of the federal courts required a substantial investment by southern states because black schools had fallen into such poor condition from lack of adequate funding over the years. But the southern states, including Florida, willingly passed such school initiatives to avoid the threat of public school desegregation and the concurrent desegregation of their societies.

At the local level in Florida, civic leaders and law enforcement officials, often in concert with white militants, also took steps to make sure that segregation barriers remained intact. Throughout the state, county sheriffs assisted grove owners, lumber, and agricultural interests in forcing black veterans to shed their uniforms and return to work in the groves and fields. Deputies often jailed blacks who expressed dissatisfaction with wages and working conditions, and they systematically assisted local leaders in repressing black desires for equality and greater freedom. When black activists persisted in their protests, they were incarcerated and often beaten until they agreed to return to work or to conform to segregation customs. In a few places, such as Lake County, deputies did not hesitate to murder particularly recalcitrant blacks as a message to others.

A revitalized Ku Klux Klan emerged in this post–World War II period as a backlash against the economic, political, and cultural changes sweeping through Florida, although the Klan was probably unnecessary because local officials and law enforcement officers were committed to the same goals. Klan leaders and their police allies, a number of whom were members of the local klaverns in Brevard and Orange counties, murdered Harry T. Moore, state leader of the NAACP, and his wife, Harriet, in their home on Christmas Eve 1951. Moore became a Klan target after he led a statewide campaign to increase black voter registration and organize black voters under one banner in Florida. In response to Moore's assassination, Governor Warren, reflecting the state's racial mores, supported only a perfunctory inquiry, and no charges resulted. An FBI-led inquiry into Moore's death, however, uncovered a widespread conspiracy of local officials, police, and militant whites in central Florida to murder the Moores and to suppress evidence against those involved in their deaths.[6] The FBI also found a far-reaching effort to repress the rights of blacks in the region. No legal action was ever taken against any official, however, and Moore's killers never went to trial, because the federal government lacked the authority to prosecute them.

Racial Change and the Collapse of Southern Leadership

The efforts of political leaders in the state to prevent racial change were gradually undermined by the federal courts, and, ironically, by the politicians' own initiatives to diversify the state's economy and increase its population. Beginning with the U.S. Supreme Court's decision against the southern white primary in 1944, the justices steadily undermined the legal foundations supporting segregation. In Florida the state's new inhabitants indirectly supported the Court's decisions. Business leaders and residents who came predominantly from the Northeast and Midwest had no interest in allowing a commitment to what they viewed as a long-dead southern past to jeopardize their businesses. They criticized the violence of the Klan and insisted that their elected officials ensure a stable environment for business. All this worked against the efforts of the rural, North Florida–dominated legislature to preserve segregation. By the late 1940s and throughout the 1950s proponents of traditional southern values squared off against new residents who sought to build a "new" Florida. Ironically, Pogo's dictum that "we have seen the enemy and he is us" was especially true in Florida as policies that emphasized economic development and population growth steadily eroded racial and social traditions.

Despite the massive growth of Florida's population during the post–World War II era, the state's racial politics and southern culture changed slowly. Commenting on the failure of these new arrivals to affect the course of Florida politics during this period, U.S. senator Bob Graham, a native of Miami, pointed to what he called the "Cincinnati factor."[7] In Graham's view many of those who had moved to Florida remained Cincinnatians in every other way. For example, they returned to Cincinnati at least once a year to visit family and friends; often sent their children to colleges in Ohio; subscribed to a Cincinnati newspaper; voted only to oppose new taxes, which they had resented when they lived in Cincinnati; and, at the end of their lives, had their remains shipped to Cincinnati for burial. Florida just happened to be the place where they lived out their senior years. This mentality significantly handicapped the ability of newcomers to transform Florida's racial and cultural traditions and to address the problems that resulted from the massive growth in South Florida.

During the 1950s the issues of race and reapportionment became inextricably linked and threatened to derail the state's population growth and economic advancement. Legislative leaders from North Florida reasoned that South Floridians did not share their commitment to the state's racial traditions and would readily cast these traditions aside if their economic prosperity and well-being were threatened. They were right. The war over reapportionment had great significance for the future of Florida, for its political environment, and for black Floridians.

As the battle unfolded, rural legislators formed the so-called Pork Chop Gang. Although journalists and political scientists often portrayed porkchoppers as representing rural North Florida and the Panhandle, most came from small counties scattered throughout the state. In fact, they often referred to themselves as the "small county coalition." These small counties were able to control the state legislature because of the way the House of Representatives was apportioned. Regardless of the population, every county could count on at least one House member, and the large counties had no more than three. From 1945 to 1965 apportionment guaranteed the small counties at least fifty seats, while the rapidly expanding urban counties seldom had more than twenty-five.

The porkchoppers "took a blood oath to stick together, and did that on all legislation," especially on reapportionment.[8] They did so to preserve Florida's heritage, as they defined it, against the invasion of newcomers. Despite the continued dramatic growth of the state, rural legislators blocked reapportionment, and the legislature remained among the worst apportioned in the nation, with a mere 13.6 percent of the state's population electing more than half the state senators, and only 18 percent of the population electing more than half the members of the House of Representatives. Governor LeRoy Collins (1955–61), elected in 1954 with substantial backing from the urban communities and with especially strong support from South Florida to fill the unexpired term of the late governor Dan McCarty, made legislative reapportionment

one of his top priorities. He introduced reapportionment in every legislative session during his six years in office, only to see it blocked by the
small county coalition.

Halfway through the two-decade reapportionment fight, the issue of
public school desegregation erupted. When the Supreme Court announced its decision in *Brown v. Board of Education of Topeka* on May
17, 1954, few in Florida anticipated what the ruling would be. Pork
Chop elements in the state legislature quickly seized the initiative, de-
nouncing the decision and drafting proposals calling for massive resistance to the court-ordered scheme. Representatives from South Florida,
the so-called Lamb Chops, generally criticized the Court's pronounce-
ment as well, but they found themselves and their state being dragged
along by North Florida politicians who militantly rejected any compromise with the Court on this issue.

When the ruling in *Brown* came down, Collins was a state senator
struggling to win the governorship in a special election, and he pledged
his commitment to segregation and said little else. As a southern business progressive, however, Collins was not an extremist. Indeed, he
actively promoted a pro-business climate so that the state would continue to diversify economically. He feared that racial militancy would
undermine his programs to modernize Florida. Moreover, as a native,
Collins was not eager to see the ambitions of his state and its future
ruined once again. Still, he was not prepared for political reasons to
accept desegregation at this point, and he joined with other southern
leaders in opposing the Court decision. He also found himself boxed in
by his leading political opponent, interim governor Charlie Johns, a
porkchopper, who denounced the Court's decision and promised to
block desegregation of the public schools by every means possible.

Once in office Collins pursued a variety of measures that were designed to preserve school segregation while he sought to avoid racial
extremism. His leadership was not as transparent or as cynical as some
northern observers initially contended. Collins well understood that
the militants would outmaneuver him and other Florida moderates
unless he proceeded carefully. North Florida had many politicians like
Charlie Johns who were prepared to embrace extremist approaches.
Moreover, they controlled the state legislature. Collins's moderate ap-

proach encountered a series of strong challenges from Johns and other Florida legislators who proposed, in the event of school desegregation, to close the schools, fund a separate private school system, and enact a measure that would block implementation of the Supreme Court's decision in Florida. Collins, however, was able to keep the racial militants at bay, thanks to the legislative calendar and his use of the veto: The legislature met only biennially during this period. His leadership helped Florida gain a reputation for racial moderation. Toward the end of his governorship Collins embarked on an educational campaign to persuade white Floridians that desegregation was only right and proper and that the state would benefit materially by accepting such change. "We can never stop Americans from hoping and praying," he told Floridians, "that someday this ideal that is embedded in our Declaration of Independence . . . that all men are created equal, that somehow will be a reality and not just an illusory goal."[9]

Collins found allies for his moderate approach in the business community and among South Floridians generally, and this support gave him the political strength that he needed to defeat the extremists. Few among the recent arrivals had a personal or economic commitment to segregated schools and a segregated society. Collins repeatedly warned Floridians that racial discrimination could cripple the state's prosperity, its postwar modernization program, and its population growth. Events proved Collins correct. During this period both population growth and tourism slowed. Given a choice between the racial unrest in Florida and the South and a tranquil environment somewhere else, tourists went elsewhere. Collins's leadership proved crucial, allowing the state to avoid the worst excesses of this era of massive resistance and sparing Florida the economic devastation experienced by Arkansas, Alabama, Mississippi, and Georgia, where the segregationists took control of state politics. As business leaders and residents of South Florida looked to the future, they realized the merit of Collins's argument and worked with him to end the state's commitment to racial discrimination. Due principally to the leadership of Collins, Florida emerged with a reputation as one of the few progressive states in the South.

Although the state lost the political skill of LeRoy Collins to term limits in 1960, its massive population growth, burgeoning tourist economy, and expanding civil rights movement continued to seed change. Collins's successors, Farris Bryant (1961–65) and Haydon Burns (1965–67), were closely allied with conservative elements in the Democratic Party and worked with rural North Florida legislators to prevent further changes to the state's racial traditions. Yet as Bryant and Burns fought to block school desegregation, they simultaneously pursued efforts to attract new businesses into Florida. These businesses insisted upon a stable economic and political environment before they would consider relocating their enterprises. Burns coordinated the recruitment of Walt Disney Productions to Orlando in the mid-1960s, and it was Disney and the other megatourist companies that further undermined racial extremism and the social instability that accompanied it. In conversations with political leaders Disney officials emphasized the company's need for a tranquil environment to ensure that tourists visited their resort. They were not proponents of racial change, but they pointed out that racial violence and social instability hurt tourism and harmed the state economically. Racial unrest in Little Rock, Arkansas, in 1957 and in St. Augustine in 1964 graphically illustrated the point. In both instances racial clashes hurt the local economies tremendously, and both communities felt the consequences of the violence for many years thereafter. For example, the media and tourists virtually ignored St. Augustine's celebration of its four-hundredth anniversary in 1965. Disney World, which opened its doors in 1971, and other tourist-oriented businesses lobbied state politicians to do whatever was necessary to avoid further racial unrest.

Although the leadership of Collins and the state's commitment to economic development eroded support for segregation and racial extremism, there was no direct evidence that Florida would be able to alter its racial traditions without intervention by the federal government. In the mid-1960s, Washington removed the civil rights issue from state control by adopting the Civil Rights Act of 1964 and the Voting Rights Act of 1965. The two laws abolished segregation in all areas of public life and ended voting restrictions based on race. The Supreme Court also ordered the implementation of the principle of one person, one vote in Florida in 1967 and, with the stroke of a pen, dismantled opposition to reapportionment.[10] Once again the federal government had stepped in to enhance Florida's future.

The actions by the federal government and the federal courts ended the stranglehold that North Florida and its political representatives had over Florida. In the wake of the Supreme Court decisions of the 1960s, the balance of power shifted to the high-growth areas of South and Central Florida, and the political, economic, and cultural orientation of these regions would shape the future of the state. One of the most dramatic eras in Florida history had ended, liberating not only black Floridians but the entire state. Florida was finally free to begin addressing issues that had been ignored during the racial crisis and that had been spurned by porkchoppers.

The Post–Civil Rights Era and Florida's Population Explosion

Florida's population growth continued its dramatic expansion in the 1970s and 1980s. The state was in the process of being transformed, fulfilling the ambitions of most natives. Yet no one in Florida had anticipated the magnitude of the population growth and its ramifications for the state. For example, neither state nor local officials had developed plans to cope with growth. Floridians confidently assured one another that they would not re-create the automobile-scarred and environmentally damaged states of New Jersey and New York, but, with almost no planning at the state or regional levels, that is precisely what they did along Florida's southeast corridor. Complicating efforts to develop plans for this growth, many of those migrating into the state often did not stay in any one community for long. Many arrived in Miami and southeast Florida, only to leave six months to a year later to seek better jobs or housing elsewhere. The state's public schools felt the brunt of this migration as enrollments fluctuated wildly from one year to the next.

Florida's population was fundamentaly transformed in the 1960s with the unexpected arrival of thousands of Cubans. In 1960 approximately 45,000 Cuban Americans lived in the state; 30,000 had been born in Cuba. Between 1960 and 1970 more than 200,000 Cubans joined the earlier émigrés in Florida, fleeing the communist oppression of Fidel Castro, who had seized power in Cuba in 1959. The immigration of Cubans put Florida on the front line of the cold war. According to the scholars Raymond A. Mohl and George E. Pozzetta, "The refugees became the prime weapon in the political war between the United States and Cuba."[11]

Fortunately for Cuban immigrants and for Florida, the United States could not afford to have these émigrés to Miami fail. The federal government provided substantial resources to ease their adjustment to U.S. society and facilitate their success. But the Cuban refugees also brought with them education, job skills, and wealth that secured their prosperity in Miami and enhanced their contributions to the state. Their settlement gradually reshaped the ethnic and cultural life of Miami and Dade County and, in the process, enabled Miami to become a financial, economic, and cultural center for the Caribbean basin. The transition of these immigrants was remarkably smooth, but the region struggled mightily and often unsuccessfully to accommodate the massive influx of residents and still preserve its quality of life.

The opening of Disney World in 1971 and the emergence of the Orlando area as a tourist mecca added to the flood of newcomers, as millions of middle-class Americans brought their children to see Mickey Mouse and friends. Orlando went from being a small town to a dynamic, sprawling metropolis with nearly 100,000 residents, and its economy shaped the entire region. Between 1971 and 1994 more than one billion people visited Disney World and the greater Orlando area. These developments, and the national and international advertising that promoted tourism, led to a population boom and urban sprawl that reshaped this region and further redefined the state.

In the brief thirty years from 1940 to 1970, Florida underwent a number of remarkable changes. Gone were the segregation laws that had determined its race relations and shaped its culture. Gone too was the political dominance of North Florida. Central and South Florida had become the dynamic regions of the state, and their political representatives finally had assumed leadership of the state legislature. Tourism and a service economy had surpassed agriculture as the state's principal economic activities. And Florida's sprawling population had taken on a new cast with the immigration of Cubans, who were the first wave of what would become a steady stream of immigrants from Latin America into the Sunshine State.

chapter 3

A Changing Population and a Changing Florida

The shifting political winds and the evolution in the state's social and cultural values permanently transformed Florida in the last quarter of the twentieth century. The emergence of South Florida as the dominant region meant that Florida would never be the same again. The residents of this region had little or no understanding of the state's cracker heritage, a limited understanding of its southern heritage, and certainly no interest in continuing either. They had built a new life for themselves in Florida, and they would in the process build a new Florida. The results of the transformation were almost immediate as voters from this region and their political representatives focused on issues that had long gone unattended.

The new era began symbolically in 1966 with the election of Claude Kirk, Florida's first Republican governor in the twentieth century. Despite his unpredictable behavior, Kirk proved to be a staunch advocate for environmental protection. He championed, in particular, the effort to stop the construction of the Cross-Florida Barge Canal. Offered as a way to link East and West Florida commercially and also to make Florida a hub of sea traffic passing from the Gulf of Mexico to the Atlantic and back, the canal gradually lost support when Floridians became aware of the potential damage to its drinking and recreational waters if a major shipping accident occurred. Kirk's leadership was instrumental in gaining the support of President Richard Nixon, a fellow Republican who spent his vacations in Florida and who observed firsthand the fragile nature of the state's environment. Nixon blocked funding measures to keep the canal alive, and eventually Florida's congressional delegation recognized that the canal should not be supported.[1]

Kirk's role in halting the Cross-Florida Barge Canal signaled the growing prominence of a politically influential environmental movement in Florida that owed much of its strength to the activism of women and the increasing prominence of South Florida in state politics. Often relegated to the netherworld of Florida politics, women struggled to find a public place in what men viewed as their domain. The "good ol' boy" world of Florida politics deemed family issues and education as realms in which women's activity was socially appropriate. But this was not sufficient for many talented and well-educated women, and those like May Mann Jennings, Marjory Stoneman Douglas, Marjorie Carr, and Gloria Rains spoke out against the degradation of Florida's environment by business interests and the state's unquestioning commitment to growth. May Mann Jennings served as a pioneer for women's and environmental issues until her death in 1963, and her efforts found resonance with Douglas, Carr, and Rains in the post–World War II era. In their writings and public addresses these women provided the impetus for the environmental movement in the state and in the process gave women an increasingly important voice in state politics.

The leadership of these environmentally conscious women enabled South Florida to overcome the laissez-faire policies of rural North Florida political leaders, most of whom were strong supporters of growth for their region. North Florida did not face the threat to its drinking water, wildlife, environment, and beaches that South Florida did from massive unregulated growth. Indeed, residents of North Florida sought such growth for their largely stagnant region.

Spurred on by Douglas and Carr, environmental politics took hold in South Florida and extended its reach to the state capitol when Reubin Askew, a Democrat, assumed the governorship in 1971. Askew (1971–79) persuaded the legislature to pass the Oil Spill and Pollution Control Act in 1970 and the Environmental Protection Act in 1971. He also sponsored a statewide conference on water management that awakened Floridians to the precarious nature of their water supply and the potential for a water crisis in southern sections of the state if growth and urban sprawl continued without regulation. In 1972 state legislators adopted the Land and Water Management Act and the Water Resources Act; together with the State Comprehensive Planning Act of 1975, these measures provided a framework for state development while attempting to protect the state's freshwater supply and its environment. Under Askew, Florida also launched a land acquisition program to preserve some of its most sensitive and endangered lands.[2] Ultimately, however, this framework proved to be little more than a levee as massive growth in the southern and central regions of the state overwhelmed efforts to protect the environment and water supply.

Bob Graham, a Democratic state senator from Dade County in South Florida and an ally of Askew's, succeeded him as governor and built upon his environmental initiatives. As the first governor from Miami in the twentieth century, Graham (1979–87) expressed his personal concerns about development patterns in South Florida and their consequences for the environment. Emphasizing the urgency of the region's environmental needs with programs entitled "Save Our Everglades" and "Save Our Coastline," Graham persuaded many Floridians to embrace the protection and acquisition of environmentally sensitive lands. Graham also styled himself as the "education governor" and sought to combine educational reform with his business recruiting efforts to broaden economic opportunities for Floridians.

Despite the progressive leadership of Askew and Graham, Florida's demographics changed so dramatically in the 1970s and 1980s that the state's growth and increasing diversity overwhelmed most political initiatives. These were, unquestionably, the most dynamic years for Florida in the twentieth century. Northerners and immigrants from Latin America flooded into the state at a rate of 842 per day for this twenty-year period (the average per day in the 1980s was 874, and the number reached more than 1,000 in the mid-1980s). The state's ability to accommodate these newcomers effectively while meeting the needs of other residents was severely strained. Urban sprawl affected and in some cases overwhelmed social services, public schools, natural resources, the environment, and local governments. Double and triple sessions became the pattern in many school districts, especially in southeast Florida and the greater Orlando area. The rate of growth slowed only slightly in the 1990s, to approximately 834 new arrivals per day. It was still a staggering figure, but a strong economy allowed the state to respond more effectively to the demands of its population growth after the crisis management of the 1970s and 1980s.

Commenting on the consequences of this dramatic population growth for the state, Lt. Gov. Buddy MacKay, a Florida native, referred to the state in the 1990s as "more of a crowd than a community."[3] The historian Michael Gannon echoed MacKay, noting that population growth had led to "a collection of cities in search of a state."[4] Whatever the appellation used to describe Florida in this period, all agreed that the rapidity and dramatic size of the population growth had changed Florida fundamentally and had severely eroded a sense of community. What the result would be, no one could be certain.

As its population expanded and became increasingly diverse after 1960, Florida's demographic features began to more closely resemble those of the Sunbelt states of Texas, Arizona, and California than those of its traditional neighbors in the South. Migration and immigration into these states and within them became a central aspect of life. Housing and roads spewed across the landscape to accommodate newcomers, creating a suburban sprawl that added to the isolation of newcomers and further eroded the environment. Instead of planting 100 more trees to the acre, grove owners found it more profitable to plant four Yankees to the acre.

As a result of the dramatic population growth, Florida's economy became increasingly dependent on housing, road construction, and tourism. Although Cape Canaveral meant that Florida literally would become a launching pad for space exploration, the space coast failed to serve as an incubator for new technology, because most basic research for space exploration was conducted in Texas and California. Advanced technology and tourism seemed to be a poor match, and the new technology companies initially showed little interest in Florida. Agriculture and, to a lesser extent the phosphate industry, cattle ranching, and the sugar industry, also felt the effects of the burgeoning population and suburban sprawl. While they remain prominent components of the state economy, their relative influence has continued to decline as agricultural lands become too valuable for farming and as newcomers oppose phosphate mines near their homes and businesses.

The growth of Florida's senior citizen and Latin American populations has led Florida's population expansion since 1970. In 1940 the
state's seniors constituted only 6.9 percent of the population, or
131,217 people. By 1970 the percentage had more than doubled, to
14.6 percent, and the actual number had increased to nearly one million people. Today Florida's seniors represent 18.5 percent of the population, or nearly three million people (2,843,497)—only West Virginia
has a greater percentage of senior citizens. Traditionally a place of
youth and beauty, Florida had suddenly become a state for growing old
and dying. It is a sea change in the way the nation views Florida and in
the way Florida sees itself. The historian Gary Mormino has reminded
Floridians that "no society had ever confronted or conceived a future in
which a large part of its population lived for two or more decades after
they stopped working."[5] The consequence of this change has extended
even to business. Eastern Airlines, for example, delayed its bankruptcy
in the 1990s by delivering coffins from southeast Florida to various
parts of the United States, and Delta Airlines transported more than
40,000 coffins from Florida alone in 1998.[6]

Seniors came to Florida because of the weather, the environment,
low taxes, and relatively inexpensive property. The weather and the
environment offered them a lifestyle that enhanced their senior years,
and the tax structure enabled most to live comfortably on their fixed
retirement incomes. H. Irwin Levy, a West Palm Beach attorney, observed the growing number of seniors in his area and launched the
massive Century Village in Palm Beach County. Built on 685 acres in
1968, Century Village became the model for other retirement villages
throughout South Florida in which as many as fifteen thousand retirees
live together. Seniors have generally settled along the southeast or
southwest coasts of Florida, with the Sarasota and Naples areas becoming the most popular in recent years.

The state's seniors have made their presence felt at the state and local
levels of government, taking an active role in the political process and
voting at much higher rates than other voters. Many early retirees who
arrived in the 1950s and 1960s were New Dealers and, as a consequence, loyal Democrats, for much of their adult lives. They continued
to support the party in Florida and became known as the "condo com-

mandos" in the Fort Lauderdale and West Palm Beach region for their ability to turn out the vote for Democratic candidates. Over time, as new retirees entered the state, Democratic loyalties began to diminish. Many younger retirees came from the Midwest and tended to be more conservative in their political views. They helped spark the resurgence of the Republican Party in the state. Finding the party's conservative positions on social, cultural, and fiscal matters more to their liking, they lent their support to Florida's disciples of Ronald Reagan. Mac Stipanovich, a Republican pollster, observed that the younger seniors had already been uprooted once, so stability became important in their new location. "That leads to a drawbridge mentality," he told the *Miami Herald*, "that once they've come here, they don't want anybody else to come along and spoil it."

Perhaps not surprisingly, senior citizens have made heavy demands on the state's social and medical services while pressuring state politicians to limit new tax initiatives and other revenue measures that might adversely affect their fixed incomes. Thus while they have supported programs to aid the infirm, provide better health care, and protect the elderly from crime, they have generally resisted new taxes for other community initiatives, including public schools. Often isolated from other citizens of Florida in gated communities or in retirement villages, they have engaged in remarkably little dialogue with other age groups. The so-called Cincinnati factor has also kept them from investing much interest or money in Florida and in programs to meet the needs of its other citizens.

The second major element in Florida's post-1960 population growth has been its diversification, led by Cuban and other Hispanic immigration. Florida has always been a destination for Latin Americans, although not necessarily a permanent one. West Indians often came into the state in the nineteenth and twentieth centuries to work in the cigar industry, in agriculture, and in railroad construction. Today Florida's Cuban-American and Latin American populations account for nearly 16.8 percent of the population, or 2,688,000 people, and they have created a more permanent place for themselves in the state. Cuban Americans constitute approximately 7 percent of the Hispanic population in Florida. Like senior citizens, Cubans quickly became a powerful political as well as an economic and cultural force in Dade County and in Florida. They have focused their political attention primarily on foreign affairs in an effort to unseat Castro, but they have also been strong advocates of an unfettered American capitalism, which has served them well. Beyond these political priorities, they have been generally conservative on social programs, reflecting their Roman Catholic faith and their focus on local community needs and concerns. The migration of Cubans and other Hispanic peoples into southeast Florida from Central America and the Caribbean has also significantly expanded the state's business influence into the Caribbean basin and Latin America.

The size of the Hispanic community has added a new ethnic dynamic to public life in Florida. Cuban Americans have followed the example of Jewish Floridians, who have lobbied frequently on behalf of Israel, in focusing on the needs of their homeland. The emergence of this ethnic Cuban dynamic has in turn marginalized racial concerns that had dominated Florida politics and social life for much of the nineteenth and twentieth centuries. With the passage of federal laws ending legal discrimination in Florida and the integration of public schools, race relations and the needs of black Floridians became much less potent issues. And Hispanics asserted their political importance by voting in much larger numbers than black Floridians, although the Hispanic community is only slightly larger. As a consequence, this political engagement has given Hispanics and Cubans in particular a more influential voice in state and local politics and, at the same time, pushed the interests of black citizens to the background in the 1980s and 1990s. This situation appears to be changing, however, as a result of One Florida and the 2000 election, which angered and reenergized black voters.

The sudden emergence of seniors and Cubans to positions of political prominence in the state both contributed to MacKay's view of Floridians as an shapeless crowd and added a tribal dimension to state politics. Florida has become sharply divided by interest groups and by regions, with voters often expressing concern about their own self-interest and showing little or no concern for the other citizens of the state. Some of this, of course, is the result of the constant arrival of so many new voters who have little understanding of the history of Florida or the issues facing the state. But much more of it is owed to certain regional, ethnic, and racial dynamics that undermine a statewide consensus. Jews and Cuban Americans, as noted, have occasionally focused more of their attention on Israel and Cuba than on Florida. Seniors have demanded state programs to address their needs and opposed additional measures that require new taxes.

Moreover, as noted in the introduction, residents of the state's various regions and cities share little in common with those in other sections of the state. Residents of Orange County (the Orlando area), for example, recognize few similarities between themselves and the Cuban-American population of southeast Florida. They also have little interest in state government and developments in Tallahassee, because Orange County is largely self-sufficient and requires minimal assistance from Tallahassee. As a consequence, Orlando-area residents are quite satisfied with their lot and see little need for a statewide approach to most issues—with the notable exceptions of public education and transportation. The same is true for residents of Miami, who have little in common with residents of North Florida and who believe that their respective interests are often diametrically opposed.[7]

Florida's unique system of state government has further exacerbated the state's cultural and geographic fragmentation. Florida's cabinet system disperses executive authority in ways that no other state does. Although voters typically view the governor as responsible for the state's far-flung bureaucracy, in reality many parts of the administration are outside the governor's control or are at best the joint responsibility of the governor and cabinet. Until the constitutional revisions of 1998, most of which were to take effect in 2002, the governor had only collegial control of public education, state land acquisition, regulation of water use, insurance regulation, and many other critical state functions. Even after the 1998 revisions, which reduced the cabinet to three officers (the secretaries of agriculture and finance and the attorney general), executive authority remains widely dispersed. Inevitably, this has created an imbalance in power between the legislative and executive branches and makes it difficult for Florida's leaders to rise above local concerns to address the long-term needs of the state as a whole.

During the 1980s and 1990s Democrats and Republicans were locked in a titanic struggle for political control of state politics, a situation that promoted a political environment in which few leaders were willing take a stand on any of the major statewide issues. When Republican governor Bob Martinez (1987–91) attempted to do so in the 1980s by calling for a new state services tax that would ensure growth in state revenues to address the burgeoning needs of Florida, members of his own party roundly condemned him—and the opposition party and a variety of special interest groups in the state piled on. The message was clear—until one party had established itself as the majority party, political leaders would shy away from initiatives as controversial as the services tax.

The consequence of such divisiveness was profound for Florida in the recession of the early 1990s. In 1992, for example, Florida was unable to staff two of its newly constructed prisons for lack of money, despite grave concerns about crime. Because of overcrowded conditions the federal courts required the state to release many felons before it could imprison new ones. In 1995 Florida ranked last in the nation in funding for higher education because Floridians were opposed to new taxes of any variety, and the state ranked near the bottom in a host of categories that related to the well-being of children. At the same time temporary classrooms surrounded local schools in every county to accommodate the growing student population. These temporary buildings scarred the local landscape, much like billboards marred Florida's highways. The expression "thank God for Mississippi" echoed in the state capitol as political leaders saw Florida falling further and further behind the rest of the nation, with only Mississippi keeping it from ranking dead last in several statistical categories.

The end of the recession in the mid-1990s and the emergence of a Republican majority in the state legislature after the 1994 election opened a new era in the state. The end of the cold war and the explosion of technology and international commerce have resurrected Florida's economy. Tourism reached an all-time high in 1999, the technology industry expanded in Central Florida, and global trade increased substantially in southeast Florida, helping to shrink statewide unemployment to less than 5 percent. A successful lawsuit brought by the state against the tobacco industry pumped an additional $11.3 billion into the state treasury. In addition, a strong economy and continued population growth provided the state with a growth dividend to pay for many of its needs. A strong Republican Party structure fostered the rise of many attractive young candidates, led by Jeb Bush, who narrowly lost the gubernatorial contest to the political icon Lawton Chiles in 1994. Despite his defeat, Bush helped state Republicans capture many local and state offices, and he ascended to the governorship in 1999. Republicans leaders reflected the new optimism in Florida. Mayor John Delaney of Jacksonville captured that sentiment when he asserted, "I would rather have the problems associated with growth than those resulting from no growth. I have lived in Cincinnati and Jacksonville. I'll take Jacksonville."[8] Delaney and an increasing number of mostly Republican mayors have been at the forefront of a movement to save the growth dividend and formulate plans that redevelop the inner city, ensure orderly growth and development, preserve and restore green space, and enhance the natural environment.

These mayors may well be leading a movement that finally offers Florida a meaningful future and ends its "throw-away" mentality, but the state's economy continues to rest on a shaky foundation of low-paying service jobs and tourism. And state revenues are based on an equally flimsy sales tax and a lottery program. Florida's political leaders have yet to find a way to attract high-paying skilled jobs, and they have been unwilling to tackle the tax structure. Florida currently ranks forty-fourth in the nation in the percent of its personal income spent on public schools, forty-seventh in higher education, forty-first in total spending, and forty-seventh in state employees per capita.[9] The state's inability to systematically address such fundamental problems as education, quality of life for children, and environmental needs persists and is unlikely to be resolved by a growth dividend alone. A more systematic approach seems essential to devising long-term solutions to such major issues.

Moreover, the tremendous growth of Florida since the end of World War II replaced a rural Deep South identity with no identity at all. Floridians have little sense of themselves as a people, and those who live in Key West and those who live in Pensacola have little in common. The absence of such a statewide or even a regional identity has limited the ability of Florida's political leaders to address its needs. Equally worrisome is the potential for a political tribalism in which ethnic, racial, religious, and age groups lobby for their own self-interests and ignore the larger needs of the state and their communities. Indeed, Florida has been a prototype for the experiences of other fast-growing states in the Sunbelt and in the South. That is why experts note that as Florida goes, so goes the Sunbelt and the fast-growing southern states. But as Florida enters the twenty-first century, the only thing that seems certain is that it will continue to see its environment deteriorate, its infrastructure stretched beyond limits, and its population grow ever larger and increasingly grayer and more diverse.

World War II unified Floridians in a way that few other events in the twentieth century have. In this photograph at the Florida State College for Women, the students called on Floridians and Americans to rally behind the nation and buy bonds.

With the outbreak of World War II over 2 million Americans came to Florida to train for the war. Veteran navigators from Pan American World Airways served in Miami as instructors for fledgling navigators at Dinner Key Base.

In an effort to persuade Americans to buy bonds to support the war effort, the federal government brought the nation's arms to communities. This photograph was taken in Leesburg, Florida in 1943.

Jacksonville, in the northeast corner of the state, developed more slowly than communities in the southern regions of Florida. Most people coming to Florida drove past the city as they headed south to West Palm Beach, Ft. Lauderdale, and Miami, and they were happy to do so to escape the smell from the paper mills. But Jacksonville had begun to modernize in the late 1950s and 1960s as this photograph indicates.

Downtown Miami offered spectacular views of the bay and the ocean, but as development took hold its image frayed. The standard array of urban problems entered everyday living: overcrowding, urban sprawl, racial divisions, and slums. And as Cubans fled communist Cuba, Miami became an immigrant and an ethnic community, a role for which it was ill prepared.

A photograph of Clearwater in the 1950s looking toward the Gulf of Mexico reveals the newness of its buildings and the urban sprawl of its development. World War II changed Clearwater and Florida forever.

By the mid-1950s, many northerners came to Florida to retire, and the state became known in some quarters as God's waiting room. Few photographs capture this aspect of the massive post–World War II migration into the state as well as this one showing seniors playing shuffleboard in Sunshine Park in Orlando.

It quickly became apparent to developers that Florida's environment was highly suitable for golf courses, and, as the game grew in popularity, they incorporated golf courses into new neighborhoods. The tourist industry also used golf to lure the rich and middle class to Florida for get-away vacations. Today, golf is one of the major tourist attractions in the state.

Pictures of attractive young women and tanned and handsome young men on Florida's gorgeous beaches were sent north to lure Yankees south during the dead of winter. And it worked.

Visitors interested in Florida's great outdoors were attracted by the state's teeming waters, and most believed they too could catch fish this size if given the chance. Fishing in the lakes and ocean is still one of Florida's great drawing cards for tourists.

The image of an environmentally pristine Florida continued to dominate the American imagination well after massive population growth had begun to change the state, and pictures like this one added to the tremendous lure of Florida.

Well before Disney World opened its facilities in Orlando in the early 1970s, tourists came to resorts like Cypress Gardens. It was the enormous appeal of Cypress Gardens that persuaded Disney and the other mega-tourist companies to locate in the state. Tourism enriched the state and attracted many Americans to move permanently to Florida.

One of the first groups of Cuban refugees arrives at Miami International Airport as part of the airlift from communist Cuba in 1961.

Many Cubans who were unable to take advantage of the airlift fled Cuba by whatever means available. Throughout the 1960s, Cubans arrived in a variety of boats, risking life and limb for freedom.

chapter 4

A View of the Twenty-first Century in Florida

"Where do these people keep coming from?" a Floridian asked her next-door neighbor. "I have no idea," responded the neighbor. "Incidentally, how are your relatives in Chicago?" the neighbor inquired. "Fine," she declared, "and yours in Rhode Island?" While the story is apocryphal, it conveys the way Floridians view one another as a result of the unceasing population growth. Change seems to be the one constant in Florida. If ten Floridians were gathered in a room, seven would be from some other state. And those states extend from the Mississippi River to the Atlantic Ocean. Added to this migration into Florida is the more recent immigration from the nations of Latin America. The rate of migration and immigration is expected to slow in the first twenty-five years of this century but not significantly.

In viewing Florida's population growth in the twentieth century and the reaction of natives to it, the popular expression that the past is the best predictor of the future certainly has relevance. Although Florida natives sought population growth, economic development, and prosperity for much of the twentieth century, they have never been fully comfortable with the changes that resulted, especially in the areas of race relations, politics, and ethnic diversity. The tumultuous changes since the end of World War II are not likely to end in Florida any time soon, as we will show here, and as a consequence neither will the political, social, racial, ethnic, and intergenerational tensions that have asserted themselves during this era. Florida—a paradise barely noticed until 1940—became a paradise sought by Americans and non-Americans after World War II and a paradise threatened in the 1980s and

1990s. Will it become a paradise spurned if it continues to avoid the substantive implications of growth in the twenty-first century?

Who Are These Newcomers?

According to current population projections, Florida will rank first among the fifty states in the number of people—approximately four million—added through net internal migration between 1995 and 2025. They will be joining a substantial number of newcomers who have settled in the state since 1970. A survey conducted for Leadership Florida, an organization that recruits and trains new community leaders in the state, found in 1999 that only one in four adult Floridians was actually born in Florida. Twenty-five percent of the state's residents came from the Northeast (principally New York and New Jersey), 14.6 percent from southern states other than Florida, and 23 percent from states outside the South or Northeast (typically the Midwest). An additional 12 percent of the population immigrated to Florida from a foreign country.[1]

The percentage of Floridians who were actually born in Florida is low even in comparison to similar statistics for other high-growth states. Figure 2 compares Florida's population to comparable data for California, Texas, and Pennsylvania. In Pennsylvania 81 percent of the adult residents were born there, compared to 25 percent for Florida. Florida's native population is also much smaller than those of Texas (62 percent) and California (43 percent), both of which, like Florida, are large states that continue to experience substantial growth.

In addition to being from somewhere else, most Floridians are also relative newcomers to the state. More than half of Florida's adult residents did not live in the state before 1975. One in four, in fact, moved to Florida during the 1990s. Almost a third of the state's residents came to Florida as youngsters with their families. Another 18 percent migrated for business or employment reasons, and 10 percent came to retire.

The state's newcomers have tended to concentrate in certain regions of the state, and they often live near people who have migrated from

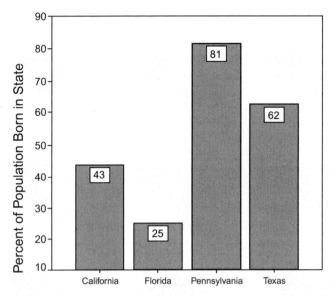

Fig. 2. Native-born population of selected states as percentage of total state population

similar sections of the country. The same Leadership Florida survey revealed the following about Florida's residents:

- The southeast coast has the highest percentage of foreign-born residents, but both the urban and rural sections of Central Florida have percentages nearly as high.
- The region with the highest percentage of northeasterners is the space coast. Northeasterners also comprise a significant part of the populations of the Tampa Bay region, urban Central Florida, and the southeast and southwest coasts.
- Midwesterners are most commonly found in southwest Florida from Naples to Tampa Bay and in northwest Florida.
- The regions with the highest percentage of native Floridians are the Tallahassee and Jacksonville areas, followed by other communities in North Florida.

The Leadership Florida survey also pointed out that most people who move to Florida develop an attachment to the state fairly quickly. Unlike those who move to Maine and are never thought of as natives, those relocating to Florida find it easy to pass as Floridians because so many are newcomers. A majority of those who have been in the state for at least a decade believe that they are in fact "Floridians." This is even true for most retirees, who, many observers have contended, develop few ties to the state and remain strongly oriented to their home states. Most newcomers to Florida, it seems, get sand in their shoes and quickly adopt the state as their own. It does not appear to matter whether they came from Georgia, Ohio, or New York or whether they moved here for work, retirement, or family reasons.

However, a significant percentage of Florida residents—more than a quarter of non-native adults—develop few emotional ties to the state. This is most often true for newcomers who for one reason or another have an overriding attachment to another place or who never intended to settle in Florida permanently. Among those who are least likely to consider themselves Floridians are college students, the unemployed, those who drift through the state, and non-Cuban, foreign-born Hispanics. The lack of connectedness to Florida by foreign-born Hispanics is significant, because they are a rapidly expanding segment of the state's population. Foreign-born Cuban Americans have adopted Florida as their home, principally because Fidel Castro has remained in power in their native land for more than four decades, and the duration of his regime has forced them to create a new life and a new community for themselves in Miami. Their situation has a permanence that is not characteristic of other Hispanic immigrants. These Latin migrants have yet to establish a similar connection with Florida because they are able to return to their homeland frequently and often do so. Many in fact have settled near airports for this reason. Instead of becoming Floridians, they remain "birds of passage" who travel back and forth between Florida and their native lands to visit family and friends and to conduct business. Their cultural ties and the way they view themselves are as much a reflection of their native lands as of their adopted land.

The transitory nature of Florida's population—so many people seem to be on their way to somewhere else—makes it exceedingly difficult to lead and to construct political coalitions to address state and local needs. The presence of a substantial number of residents who do not view themselves as Floridians creates a peculiar set of problems. These people have little concern for the issues that face Florida.

Even those who adopt Florida as home have not lived here long and typically lack perspective on the state's development. As a consequence, like those passing through, they know little about the state's history and culture and have almost no understanding of the state's needs. The Florida that they know is the one that they encountered on arrival. The overwhelming majority, for example, know nothing about the state's racial, environmental, or agricultural heritage. They do not recognize the names of LeRoy Collins or Reubin Askew, the state's two most important governors in the twentieth century, or the initiatives that they pursued as governor and why they pursued them. So, while newcomers often view themselves as Floridians, the perception has little meaning.

The state has done remarkably little to educate its children about Florida's rich history. The public school curriculum does not include a single course on Florida government. The rootlessness that characterizes a large proportion of Florida's population is not only going unaddressed but is being passed on to the next generation.

Given this situation, the natives and long-term residents would seem to be in a position to provide political direction because the newcomers are so numerous and so few of them understand the state's needs. But the natives and long-term residents are a mix of southerners, northeasterners, and midwesterners themselves and typically have little in common and are often divided by political philosophy. As a result, they lack the consensus to address the state's problems or fail to agree on political leaders who can address those issues.

Population Trends in the Twenty-first Century

As demographers assess the population projections for Florida through 2025, they believe that the pace of growth will slow somewhat and will not fluctuate quite so wildly as it did in the last half of the twentieth century. Nevertheless, growth will remain the dominant feature of life in Florida for most of the twenty-first century. As the pace of popula-

Table 3. Projected growth from 2000 to 2025

Year	Population	Population growth in decade
2000	15,982,378	3,044,452
2010	17,836,377	2,407,504
2025	20,710,000	2,873,623

tion growth eases, Florida should begin to feel less like a boomtown, with a boomtown mentality. That in itself will be a significant improvement from the past fifty years.

For the foreseeable future Florida will remain enormously appealing to many Americans and to an increasing number of non-Americans. The Florida Dream still resonates in the American psyche and has been only partially diminished by crime, overpopulation, the graying of the citizenry, and environmental damage. The state's strong economy from 1994 to 2000 in fact added to its appeal among many Americans, Latin Americans, and Europeans.

Between now and 2025, approximately 579 people are expected to enter the state every day, which adds up to approximately 2.4 million each decade (see table 3). This growth rate is considerably slower than it was in the 1980s and the 1990s. In the 1980s the growth rate averaged nearly 874 people per day, while in the 1990s the population expanded by approximately 834 people per day. But adding 579 people a day is still substantial by any measure. It is the equivalent of adding a midsize city like St. Petersburg—more than 211,000 people—every year for the first twenty-five years of the new century. And although these newcomers may quickly embrace their adopted state, they will have a limited understanding of Florida's past, the significance of the changes since World War II, and the issues that are fundamental to Florida's future, unless policy leaders are willing to educate them. But as the twenty-first century begins, neither political party seems willing to engage the public on the really difficult issues. Moreover, the parties' ability to do so is complicated by Florida's geographic fragmentation.

Racial and Ethnic Diversity by 2025

A Cuban-American resident of Miami commented recently that she does not consider North Florida to be part of her Florida.[2] She is not alone in this view. Residents of South and North Florida view one another suspiciously, often wondering, "Who are these people?" Moreover, even among whites who view the state's growing diversity as a positive development, few welcome the thought of a society that is shaped principally by a Hispanic culture and Hispanic traditions.

The rapid transition from a state that was predominantly southern to one that is increasingly diverse helps explain the perceptions of whites. Only a hundred years ago most non-native Floridians came from Georgia, Alabama, or South Carolina, and they lived within fifty miles of the Georgia-Alabama border (see chapter 1). A century later a majority of the 15.9 million Floridians live closer to the Caribbean than to Georgia, and these newcomers are a heterogeneous lot by any measure. Since 1950 people from throughout the United States and the Western Hemisphere have discovered Florida. A sociologist is fond of saying that Floridians are as different and as vibrant as a patchwork quilt, but that diversity has never been as significant or as important as it is today.

Few white or ethnic Floridians realize that the state has always had an ethnically diverse population. Italians and Cubans settled in the Tampa Bay region in the early twentieth century and spurred development of the cigar industry. Cubans and other peoples from the Caribbean also lived and fished in the Keys and Miami and helped Henry Flagler build the Florida East Coast Railway to Key West. A number of Greeks, Danes, Japanese, and Swedes settled in the state and assisted in the development of the citrus and seafood industries, in particular.

The influence of Florida's hyphenated and minority citizens is, however, significantly different today than it was in the early twentieth century. During this early period immigrants were influential only at the local level, and even there their influence was sharply restricted by the dominant white culture and by prevailing racial and ethnic prejudices. By contrast, at the beginning of the twentieth-first century, ethnic and racial minorities play a significant role in state politics, economic life,

Table 4. Origins of immigrants to Florida, 1995

Country	Number	% of total immigrants
Cuba	22,200	28
Haiti	7,700	10
Jamaica	4,900	6
Colombia	3,500	4
Nicaragua	3,400	4
Mexico	3,100	4
Peru	2,300	3
Dom. Rep.	2,000	3
Canada	1,800	2
Philippines	1,800	2
Other	26,000	33

Source: Bureau of Economic and Business Research, *Florida Statistical Abstract, 1997,* 31st ed., 65.

and regional culture. Moreover, all indicators point to the state's becoming even more diverse, and Hispanics will certainly become a dominant minority, if not the majority, in Florida, because they have made Florida one of their favorite destinations in the United States.

Florida's immigration figures for 1995 and 1998 reveal the continuing prominence of Latin American immigration into the state (see tables 4 and 5).

Although these immigration trends show no sign of abating in the twenty-first century, Cuban immigration may well lessen or stop altogether when Castro's political control of Cuba ends. Assuming a change in government will take place when he dies, Cubans and Cuban Americans will begin moving back and forth between Miami and Cuba. Cuban immigration to the United States will almost surely slow dramatically, and some Floridians of Cuban heritage will no doubt return to their native land. Nevertheless, this development may provide Florida with an even more prominent role in the Caribbean and Central America, spurring economic activity and trade between the United States and Cuba and further accelerating interest in the state among people in that region. Moreover, continuing political and economic turmoil in nations like Colombia, Jamaica, the Dominican Republic, and Haiti, just to mention a few, suggests that more people from Latin America, rather than fewer, will seek to enter Florida.

Table 5. Origins of immigrants to Florida, 1998

Country	Number	% of total immigrants
Cuba	14,300	24
Haiti	6,600	11
Jamaica	4,800	8
Colombia	3,500	6
Mexico	2,800	5
Peru	1,900	3
Honduras	1,600	3
Dom. Rep.	1,500	3
Canada	1,100	2
India	1,100	2
Other	20,800	35

Source: Bureau of Economic and Business Research. *Florida Statistical Abstract, 2000,* 34th ed., 73.

Notions of what it means to be a Floridian thus remain in flux and are certain to be further redefined over time. Florida's Hispanic population, now at 16.8 percent (slightly less than 2.7 million people), is projected to reach 24 percent (or nearly 5 million people) in 2025 (see table 6). In a 1995 article in *Population and Development Review,* demographer Douglas Massey argued that we are witnessing an age of "perpetual immigration" in which the new immigrant populations from Latin America and Asia are continually "augmented by a steady supply of fresh arrivals from abroad."[3] Moreover, the state's black population, currently at 14.6 percent (or approximately 2,336,000 people), and in steady decline as a percentage of the state's total population throughout the twentieth century, is projected to increase to 17 percent (or 3.6 million people) by 2025.

Despite the dramatic changes in its population and in the complexion of Floridians, the state will see remarkably small shifts in its racial and ethnic composition through 2025. Although Hispanics and black residents will constitute more than 40 percent of the population in 2025, the state's population will remain overwhelmingly white because a significant number of Hispanics define themselves as both Hispanic and white. Racial traditions in both Latin America and the United States account for much of this ethnic identity, with many Hispanics seeing inherent value in being perceived as both white and Hispanic.

Table 6. Ethnic groups as percentage of Florida's population

Year	White	Black	Hispanic
1995	85	13.7	14.4
2000	78	14.6	16.8
2025	79.87	17.17	23.87
2025 (in U.S.)	78.27	14.19	17.59

Note: The Hispanic category is a self-identification, and some identify themselves as both Hispanic and white.

The largest blocs of Cuban Americans are clustered in southeast Florida, especially in the Miami-Dade County area. That will probably not change a great deal between now and 2025. Immigrants tend to settle in areas that offer familiarity and community support, and most of these are near such immigrant gateways as Los Angeles, New York, and Miami. Immigrants choose gateway cities because they are near airports, an arrangement that enables them to return to their native lands frequently.

If immigration continues to be as steady as Massey believes and residential patterns continue to evolve in this manner, southeast Florida from south Dade County to Fort Lauderdale, and perhaps much of Broward County, could well become a major Latin region as immigrants from Latin America seek housing. Broward's population is more than 15 percent Hispanic, and several of Broward's cities have become predominantly Hispanic. Pockets of South American communities are likely to appear throughout other sections of the state, especially near major airports, where international business activity tends to locate. In Orlando, for example, most major international corporations have located near the airport, and developers of a few residential areas specifically target Puerto Ricans and South Americans in their advertising.

The changing complexion of Florida will continue to have significant political consequences. In 2000 Florida's voting-age population that was non-Hispanic white stood at 8.3 million, or 71.1 percent of eligible voters. Non-Hispanic blacks numbered 1.4 million, or 12.2 percent of the population; Asians and Pacific Islanders numbered 178,000, or 1.5 percent; and Hispanics numbered 1.8 million, or 15 percent of the state population. By 2025 the increase in the number of

Hispanic voters, who are expected to constitute about 24 percent of the state's population, will enable them to extend their political influence well beyond Dade County.

Some writers have argued that minorities—Hispanic and African-American voters—will dominate Florida politics in the twenty-first century. Certainly, if Hispanics join forces with black voters, they could constitute about 40 percent of the electorate in 2025. However, if Hispanics continue to define themselves as both Hispanic and white, the likelihood of a coalition of Hispanic and black voters seems remote. Moreover, Cuban-American voters today have little in common with black voters. Cuban Americans remain conservative on social issues, reflecting their Roman Catholicism and their support of American capitalism, which has served them well. In addition, most Cuban Americans remain fixated on developments in their former homeland and have focused much of their political energies on efforts to undermine the Castro regime. In none of these areas is there common ground with black voters.

Although the Cuban-American vote is comparatively small, it has been a major factor in the Republican Party's rise to power in Florida. Cuban Americans have voted as a bloc for the party, which has enabled the GOP to build a strong base of support in southeast Florida. On the eve of the 2000 elections, approximately 700,000 Hispanics were registered to vote in Florida. Of this number, nearly 385,000 were Cuban Americans living in southeast Florida. While this number may seem small, it takes on added significance because many recent elections in Florida have been decided by fewer than 100,000 votes.

Other Hispanic voters have been a minor factor in state politics, because they often do not vote. They do not yet see themselves as Floridians because they travel so frequently between the state and their native lands. Moreover, they share little in common with other Hispanic immigrants to Florida because of their continuing identity with their native lands. Colombians, Nicaraguans, and Brazilians, for example, do not see themselves as Hispanics, and they seldom interact with Mexicans, Puerto Ricans, and Haitians. Profound class differences separate these groups. Mexicans, Haitians, and Dominicans typically are poor and unskilled and work in the tourist industry and as migrant laborers. But Colombians, Nicaraguans, and Brazilians tend to be well-to-do immigrants who settle in Florida for business or investment reasons or who seek to establish residence so that they can educate their children in U.S. schools.

Despite the differences between these groups, the growth of the ethnic and racial minority population in the twenty-first century worries native whites and other white migrants, who tend to view Hispanics as one large ethnic bloc. How whites respond to the increasing number of racial and ethnic minorities will significantly influence Florida's future. Sociologists have cautioned about the emergence of "white ethnicity" in Florida.[4] The existence of several white extremist organizations throughout Florida and the state's history of racial oppression in the nineteenth and twentieth centuries suggest that racial and ethnic tensions could be explosive in the future, and incidents of racial and ethnic discrimination and physical assaults against minorities continue in Florida.

For now, however, the state's robust economy has served to calm racial and ethnic relations. Opportunities abound for most people regardless of the color of their skin, and no single group feels excessively threatened by the other. Moreover, many immigrants have been taking jobs that do not interest whites.

Nevertheless, Governor Bush's "One Florida" proposal, with its elimination of affirmative action, has driven a racial wedge into the state's body politic and revealed that sharp differences lie just beneath the surface. Whites and Hispanics generally supported the governor's initiative, but black Floridians conducted massive protests against the plan throughout the state. The opening day of the 2000 session of the Florida legislature saw the arrival in Tallahassee of 50,000 protesting the governor's proposal, the largest civil protest in Florida history. The efforts of Miami's Cuban-American community to block the deportation of Elian Gonzalez, the six-year-old refugee from Cuba, added to concerns among whites about ethnic diversity in Florida and raised additional warning flags that racial and ethnic divisions could well dominate political discourse in the new century.[5]

The Baby Boomers as Retired Citizens

Although the state's population will become increasingly diverse in the new millennium, this development will not constitute the state's most dramatic demographic development. Almost half the increase in Florida's population during the next twenty-five years will come from people who are sixty-five and older. Florida already has a large percentage of retirees, but it will pale in significance to the "age wave" that will wash across the state in the next three decades.

It seems particularly relevant that the state song, Stephen Foster's "Suwannee River," is also known as "Old Folks at Home" after the last line of its first verse. The emergence of a large and dynamic senior population has been unfolding rapidly in Florida since the early 1970s. As noted earlier, seniors represented only 6.9 percent of Florida's population in 1940, but by 1970 that figure had leaped to 17.3 percent. By 1990 ten of the nation's eleven most senior counties and fifteen of the top nineteen were in Florida. The state's retirees today constitute more than 18 percent of the population, or nearly 2.9 million people. The age groups of fifty to sixty and of eighty-five and older will be the fastest growing in Florida. The former constitute those born just before World War II separated their parents and just after the war when they were reunited (see table 7).

Table 7. Population 50 years and older in 1999 and projections for 2010

Age	Population 1999	Population 2010
50–54	931,526	1,333,152
55–60	778,008	1,249,569
60–64	708,518	1,175,267
65–69	722,377	481,241
70–74	725,947	778,897
75–79	622,936	643,894
80–84	426,539	536,250
85 and older	317,599	495,740

Source: Bureau of Economic and Business Research, *Florida Statistical Abstract, 2000,* 34th ed., 33.

Of the 20.7 million people projected to live in the state in 2025, 1.1 million will be younger than five (approximately 5 percent of the population); 2.9 million will be aged five to seventeen (approximately 14 percent); 1.5 million will be eighteen to twenty-four (approximately 7.5 percent); and 9.8 million will be between twenty-five and sixty-four (approximately 47 percent). The number of senior citizens, those older than sixty-five, is expected to be 5.5 million (26.33 percent of the population). Florida will be the oldest state in the nation; by contrast, Alaska will be the youngest, with only 10 percent of its population aged sixty-five years or older.

Florida will see its senior population virtually explode after 2010 with the retirement of the Baby Boom generation. More than half of these people will have lived in Florida for twenty years or longer when they reach retirement age—a percentage higher than that for the previous generation of retirees, most of whom came from some place other than Florida and arrived after their retirement.

The Baby Boomers, who were born between 1946 and 1964, have been moving through American society like the proverbial pig through a python. They were members of the Cleaver family in the 1950s; the civil rights demonstrators, Vietnam veterans, war protesters, and the hippies of the '60s; the yuppies of the '70s and '80s; and the soccer moms and high-tech dads of the '90s. As the nation entered the new millennium, they were fast approaching retirement. Indeed, in the United States a boomer turns fifty every seven seconds. In a few more years they will be retiring at a rapid rate, and many will choose to spend their retirement years in Florida.

The sheer numbers of Florida's senior citizens already give them an influence that few other age groups can match, because they vote in much larger numbers than other constituent groups. The U.S. Census Bureau and the state Division of Elections found that in 1998 seniors constituted 18 percent of the state's population, 24 percent of the voting-age population, and 27 percent of the state's registered voters. Furthermore, exit surveys made during the 1998 gubernatorial election revealed that seniors represented 32 percent of all voters. And when those aged sixty and older were lumped together, they represented a staggering 42 percent of the voters. In local elections in Florida those older than sixty-five occasionally comprise more than 50 percent of the electorate. In 1998, five Florida counties—Charlotte, Citrus, Highlands, Pasco, and Sarasota—had populations in which one-third were older than sixty-five. Several of the state's major urban aggregations have senior populations greater than 20 percent, including Fort Myers–Naples with 24.6 percent, West Palm Beach–Fort Pierce with 23.2 percent, and Tampa–St. Petersburg with 22.7 percent. As the political scientist Susan MacManus has pointed out, seniors are increasingly electing their own to local and county government posts. They constitute 29 percent of the city council members in Florida, for example, compared to 23 percent nationally.[6]

By 2025 as many as twenty-two of the state's sixty-seven counties are expected to have senior populations larger than 30 percent. By any measure these seniors will constitute the single most influential group in state politics. At the local level they will have the ability to decide most elections. Moreover, in statewide campaigns in nonpresidential elections, seniors in 2025 could well determine the outcomes with no assist from other groups. There seems to be little question that they will shape the political agenda and the platforms of political candidates at all levels of government. Candidates will find it virtually impossible to win without their support.

Who, then, are these Baby Boomers, and how will they influence Florida politics? From all indications Baby Boomers will differ from their parents in their political, social, and cultural values. Their parents were part of an extraordinary generation that came of age in the turmoil of the Great Depression, fought to preserve democracy in World War II, built a dynamic and generally prosperous postwar economy, and engaged in a prolonged and often terrifying confrontation with Soviet communism. Historian Stephen Ambrose says, "The 'we' generation of World War II (as in 'We are all in this together') was a special breed of men and women who did great things for America and the world. When the GIs sailed for Europe, they were coming to the continent not as conquerors but liberators."[7] Eager to preserve the freedoms that they fought so hard to defend during World War II and the cold war, this generation has been supportive of a strong military and of traditional U.S. social and cultural values.

The children of this generation, the Baby Boomers, have had a quite different life experience. In their formative years they enjoyed the relative affluence of the 1950s as their parents prospered, purchased single-family homes for the first time, and began the migration to the suburbs. With the freedom provided by their parents' economic achievements, the Baby Boomers did not have to rush out to work after high school. Indeed, their parents encouraged them to attend college. Many were the first in their family to obtain a college degree.

As the Baby Boomers matured, they were also the first generation of Americans to experience the end of what has been called the "victory culture." From the nation's beginnings Americans had thought of themselves as bringing civilization through democracy to a backward and hostile world. Members of the World War II generation fought an all-out war in good conscience, even using nuclear bombs against civilian cities in Japan, because they were convinced the cause was right. Most believed that they were fighting for democracy, freedom, and economic prosperity against the evils of fascism and totalitarianism.

But World War II and its aftermath made this victory culture problematic at best. The nuclear arms race with the Soviets and the potential for world devastation raised obvious doubts about the value of any future military victory in a war between nations. Conflagration was no longer a distant possibility; it was something that could happen at any time and literally in a flash. The Baby Boomers were repeatedly reminded of this when, as youngsters, they participated in weekly "duck-and-cover" drills at school in preparation for nuclear war. The Cuban missile crisis made the possibility of nuclear conflagration all too real, especially in Florida. When President John F. Kennedy placed a naval blockade around Cuba in October 1962 and demanded that the Soviet Union remove its nuclear missiles from the island, the world was on the brink of nuclear war.

America's pride in its national values was also put to the test by the street protests of civil rights leaders who sought to end segregation and to secure freedom and opportunity for black Americans. The violence against nonviolent demonstrators by law enforcement officials stunned Americans, black and white, in the North and in the South. As these scenes were repeated on national television, many had difficulty reconciling the treatment of black citizens with the values for which the United States had fought in World War II and the ideology of the cold war, which sought to distinguish the freedom and democracy of the United States from the totalitarianism of the Soviet Union. The nation's political leaders slowly recognized the national dilemma and eventually stepped in to guarantee the civil rights of black citizens but only after years of struggle by African Americans.

Baby Boomers also championed the women's revolution. Women of this generation discarded the role of Mrs. Ward Cleaver, who stayed at home to manage the needs of her children and husband, and sought a more complete role for themselves and their daughters in society. In the process Baby Boomer women redefined the nation's cultural and sexual values.

Finally, of course, the Boomers also were molded by Vietnam and Watergate. The United States justified its involvement in Vietnam as a campaign to defend the South Vietnamese people from the totalitarianism of communism and to halt the spread of Chinese and Soviet imperialism. As victory eluded the United States and the war effort escalated, the United States looked more and more like an imperial tyrant than a defender of democracy. Many Baby Boomers initially supported and participated in the conflict, but as the violence in Vietnam exploded on the nightly television news and men were carried away in body bags, this generation questioned the war and launched protests against it. Testifying to the collapse of the victory culture was that veterans returning from Vietnam were treated not as heroes but often as villains. Watergate added to the public questioning of the nation's political leadership and its political values, and President Richard Nixon's administration seemed to embody all that had gone wrong with the country.

Public cynicism spread throughout the nation and shook the Boomers' confidence in the future of their country. In the 1980s, following the runaway economic inflation of the previous decade and widespread self-doubt about the nation's future, many of them joined other voters in support of the Reagan revolution. They saw in Reagan a leader who could restore the nation's confidence in itself and reassert its leadership in the world.

All these experiences shaped the Baby Boomer generation and its political attitudes. Boomers are not easy to categorize, as this brief history suggests, because they are much more politically independent than their parents, and they are hardly uniform in their thinking. They tend to vote on issues and candidates rather than on the basis of party loyalty. For example, following the Reagan and Bush years of the 1980s and early 1990s, many abandoned the conservative ideology of the Republican right for the more moderate conservatism of Bill Clinton and the Democratic Party. Susan MacManus, for one, predicts that the senior vote "will be a bit more volatile in the 21st century."[8]

Although many Boomers have mellowed a great deal in middle age, they remain committed to many changes that have occurred during their lifetimes. The National Election Study, which has been conducted in all even-numbered years since 1948, suggests that the Baby Boomers, like previous generations, have become more conservative as they have grown older. This is not surprising; as the humorist Mark Twain observed, "A man who is not a liberal at twenty has no heart. A man who is not a conservative at forty has no brain." But the conservatism among Baby Boomers differs from that of their parents, because the Boomers started from a different place ideologically. In their twenties, thirties, and forties they were much more liberal on social issues than their parents. Even today, they are more likely than those in other age groups to define themselves explicitly as liberals. Their parents came of age in the Great Depression and New Deal era, and they have remained Democrats for most of their lives. The party's commitment to social security, military preparedness, and government activism reflected their life experience. Yet only 10 percent of this older generation thinks of itself as liberal. By contrast, surveys show that 25 percent of the Baby Boomers identify themselves as liberals. When compared to other adult Americans, Boomers typically express less support for the military as an institution and for programs to increase military expenditures. These attitudes are a holdover from the Vietnam era and the Boomers' cynicism about the defense establishment.

Baby Boomers also championed programs to achieve equality for African Americans and women and to protect the environment. More than all other age groups, Boomers support the integration of U.S. society and women's rights. They are also more likely than other age groups to see evidence of persistent racism in our society. Support for environmental protection is rooted in their experience with the first Earth Day in 1972 and concern about the pollution of the environment and its ramifications for the planet and for people's health. The so-called radicalism of some Baby Boomers subsided as they assumed the responsibilities of adulthood, but their idealism and passion for these policies have remained.

The Baby Boomers also generally value international political and economic cooperation. As adults they participated in and not infrequently led the transformation of the U.S. economy from industrial manufacturing to high technology, at a time when many predicted that the United States would lose its position of economic leadership to Japan. They also gradually supported globalism and international trade, believing that these would enhance prosperity and reduce the threat of nuclear confrontation and proliferation. Moreover, the concept of globalism appeals to many Boomers as they search for ways to address environmental problems that extend beyond national borders.

Because many Boomers have held on to their political ideals, retirement may see them reassert their youthful idealism. Retirement will release them from the conformist pressures of work and provide them with economic security, not unlike what they experienced as students in the 1960s. Much like their parents' generation, they are expected to be politically active. But unlike that generation, Boomers will probably have a progressive, rather than a conservative, policy orientation.

The projected social and economic demographics paint a generally positive picture for the next generation of Florida's senior citizens. With some exceptions the Baby Boom seniors are much better off financially than their parents were as they approach their retirement years. A generally strong economy has strengthened their investments and retirement portfolios. Seniors continue to come to Florida looking for tax advantages and for an environment that allows them to enjoy their final years in a pleasant climate. Thus every indication is that the Baby Boomers in 2025 will be healthier, more financially secure, and more active than any preceding generation of retirees.

Their wealth will be an asset to Florida. Although many consider seniors to be a drain on the state economy, recent studies dispute that.

Between 1985 and 1990, for example, seniors transferred $8 billion in assets to Florida and transferred only $1.8 billion out of the state. Following a county-by-county study of seniors in 1998, economist Hank Fishkind concluded, "Through spending and taxes, Florida's resident retirees not only pay their own way, they actually generate more than a billion-dollar surplus each year for the state's counties and their public school systems."[9] Others contend that seniors are the ultimate "clean industry."

The growing number of senior citizens has significant implications for public policy, especially in the areas of health care, transportation, the workplace, and social programs. In health care alone, for example, the leading causes of death in Florida are closely related to the age of its population: Heart disease tops the list at 31.5 percent of all deaths, followed by cancer at 24 percent, and cerebrovascular diseases at 6 percent. Statistics show that seniors live generally healthy lives up to age seventy-five, at which point physical disabilities begin to occur. Nevertheless, longevity for seniors will continue to improve with advances in health care, diet, and exercise. The Boomers have redefined what it means to be fifty and sixty, and they are likely to continue to redefine their senior years as they live longer and healthier lives. As we noted earlier, one of the largest and fastest-growing groups in Florida is senior citizens aged eighty-five and older. That trend is expected to continue throughout the twenty-first century. As seniors live increasingly into their eighties, nineties, and beyond, they will insist that Florida have in place a good health-care infrastructure. They will also insist on state programs to provide transportation, social programs to enhance the quality of their senior years, and medical care that will be affordable.

Will seniors continue to retire to Florida as their parents' generation did before them? As mentioned, a majority of the state's Boomers will be Floridians who have lived in the state for a significant period of their adult lives. Yet projections are also based on the large numbers of out-of-state Boomers who are expected to relocate to Florida. Whether the Boomers will do so is not clear. Many recent seniors have found the large retirement condominiums of South Florida unappealing. And as older seniors have begun dying, younger seniors have not moved in to replace them. According to some, younger retirees see Florida as a place "their parents went to retire, and these new retirees see themselves as far too young to be hanging out with that crowd of geezers." [10] Moreover, even when younger seniors do move into condo developments with older seniors, they stay only briefly, often relocating farther north. Known as "half-backs," these seniors have sought more dynamic communities in North Florida or in other southern states that take them halfway back to their former state of residence.

The evidence suggests that Florida in the new century will continue to struggle mightily with the dynamics of population growth. Since 1950, growth usually has exceeded the fondest wishes of natives, and while many benefited economically by these changes they also saw their state altered dramatically. No one anticipated the rate of growth that occurred and the changes that it would foster.

The rate of growth for Florida in the twenty-first century is now much better understood than it was at any point in the twentieth century, and the ramifications of that growth are also more obvious. Policy leaders have reasonably reliable projections showing that the state's population in 2025 will be larger, more racially and ethnically diverse, and older than it has been. How this huge population of seniors intersects with a higher proportion of both African Americans and Hispanics in Florida, not to mention younger voters, will say much about the future of state politics.

The ongoing consequences of population growth, the increasing diversity of its population, and the aging of its population require strong state and local leadership that will educate Floridians about the value of racial and ethnic diversity and that will integrate seniors into the fabric of community life. Florida government, which was reactive in the late twentieth century, must become proactive in helping citizens to address these projected developments and to ensure that such changes occur in a manner that is beneficial for Florida and for subsequent generations. But Florida's failure to assert such leadership in the past—let alone plan for the growth that has taken place—can make no one sanguine about the future.

chapter 5

The Impending Battle
over Florida's Future

Florida's modernization in the twentieth century occurred in fits and starts as people from sundry points in the United States and Latin America discovered the state and decided to make it home. Northern investors arrived in the early decades of the century, wealthy tourists in the 1920s, military troops during World War II, a flood of northeasterners and midwesterners immediately after the war, retirees in the 1960s and 1970s, and, most recently, Cubans and other Hispanics. In each instance Florida accommodated the newcomers, often with remarkable agility but not without social turmoil and conflict and not without changes to its culture, economy, politics, and government. The state's dramatic shift from one arriving population group to another has been thorny because nearly every new wave of immigrants has been large and culturally distinct from the residents they were joining. Compounding the social, cultural, and political friction generated by this layered growth has been political restrictions in Florida that made it difficult for newcomers to exert political influence commensurate with their numbers. Examples of such obstacles are the malapportionment of the legislature before 1970; an executive branch fragmented by a separately elected cabinet; at-large elections for most positions in local government, which prevented new groups from electing one of their own; gerrymandering to protect incumbents and parties during legislative redistricting; and constitutional restrictions on taxation. These factors allowed natives and long-time residents to stay in control for most of this period and block changes that newcomers sought.

In this chapter we look to the future to determine what the political and demographic trends will be and how they will affect the state. In general we have concluded that most of these patterns—population growth, the graying of Florida, increasing ethnic and racial diversity, and innate resistance to change—will continue. The political pressures to find solutions will be significant, but they will run smack into opposition to change. How such matters get resolved will say much about the state's future.

The political tensions will likely center around questions of group identity and group need. Florida's political cleavages both now and in the future will arise from differences between self-defined social groupings, with race, ethnicity, culture, and age as the dominant ones. The Florida electorate is a motley combination of African Americans, Cuban Americans and other Hispanic Americans, white southerners (and crackers), northeasterners, midwesterners, and retirees. To date, none of these groups has joined with another to form bonds of trust, much less a stable political coalition. White southerners and African Americans remain suspicious of one another. Cuban Americans see themselves and their concerns as different from other Hispanic Americans and from other Floridians. Retirees from the Midwest differ from those from the Northeast in their political and cultural values. Hispanics often identify themselves as white rather than as a racial minority, and this significantly undermines ties with African Americans. The ways in which these groups interact with one another and address their differences will shape the state's development in the twenty-first century.

Florida's Rural Politics

Newcomers who enter Florida encounter a state in which rural white voters historically have dominated its politics and still play a key role. Affectionately referred to as crackers by the late governor Lawton Chiles, this segment of the population constitutes an atavistic remnant of the antebellum South. Crackers are concentrated in the Panhandle and in the agricultural regions running down the center of the state from Ocala to Polk, Glades, De Soto, and Hendry counties. To be sure, the cracker vote in Florida is a small part of the electorate, but it retains an influence larger than its numbers because people who have migrated into Central and South Florida since the mid-1950s have only recently begun to unify as a political force.

When Florida's population boom began in 1945, the in-migrating populations brought with them conflicting political loyalties that prevented an urban coalition from forming. Settled heavily by midwesterners, the southwest coast tended to be Republican. By contrast, northeasterners, many of whom were New Deal Democrats, resided along the southeast coast.

These two groups—midwestern Republicans and northeastern Democrats—more or less balanced each other out in statewide political races, allowing the white rural conservative voters to maintain a major voice in most statewide elections, even as their numbers dwindled and the federal courts ordered reapportionment of the state legislature. Moreover, cracker representatives continued to play a prominent role in the legislature well into the 1990s, using their longevity in the legislature and their political skills to gain important committee chairmanships. That cracker voice has diminished in recent years as a result of dwindling numbers and term limits, but crackers continue to be an independent lot who can influence close elections by throwing their weight to one side or the other.

Voter Registration and Emerging Republican Dominance

Although 1999 voter registration figures showed that Florida was still a Democratic state, the growth of the Republican Party in the last decades of the twentieth century nearly closed the gap. As figure 3 shows, Republican voter registrations increased steadily during the second half of the twentieth century. In 1950 fewer than 10 percent of the state's voters were registered Republicans; by 1999 more than 40 percent of all registered voters belonged to the Republican Party. Despite these gains, Republican registration has leveled off since 1999, and Democrats continue to outnumber Republicans by almost a half-million registered voters.

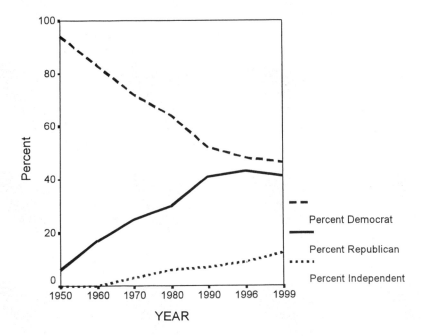

Fig. 3. Registered voters in Florida, 1950–1999

When it comes to state elections, however, the Republican Party has clearly become the dominant party in Florida. During the 1990s Republicans seized control of the governor's office for only the second time and the state legislature for the first time in the twentieth century. And as the twenty-first century began, Republicans held significant majorities in both the Florida House and the Florida Senate and controlled more than half the seats in the Florida cabinet, a majority of the state's congressional delegation, and the governor's office. Clearly, many independents and a significant number of registered Democrats have abandoned their party at the polls and voted Republican.

Moreover, the influence of term limits, and legislative redistricting, set to occur in 2002, will give the Republican Party a clear advantage. Florida enacted term limits in a 1992 amendment to the state constitution that placed an eight-year limit on all state senators, representatives, cabinet officers, and the governor and lieutenant governor. The greatest effect of term limits has been felt in the legislature. In 2000, the first year that veteran legislators were confronted by term limits, a staggering fifty-seven state representatives had to surrender their seats, as did eleven state senators. Because Republicans hold the majority, they face greater danger from term limits than Democrats. But the party appears to have greater resiliency than the Democratic Party. Republicans are much better organized in Florida and have systematically identified local leaders for political office and then groomed them for state office. The Democrats, who dominated state politics for most of the twentieth century, have historically lacked a strong party structure because they had no need for one until Republicans mounted their challenge in the 1980s. Democrats have been slow to organize in response, and they find themselves constantly on the defensive, fighting to hold ground when they should be organizing to turn the political tide.

A Republican legislature was expected to oversee legislative redistricting in 2002 and to use the process to solidify its control of the statehouse, much as Democrats did in the past. The Democrats fended off the Republican takeover of the state legislature in the 1970s and 1980s by artfully drawing legislative districts to maximize the number of Democrats who would be elected. The proportion of state Senate seats controlled by Republicans, for example, increased in the late 1960s, the late 1970s, and the late 1980s, but in each instance Democratic control of the redistricting process reversed the GOP's gains. In 1970 Republicans held fifteen seats in the Senate, but after redistricting in 1972 the number dropped to ten. By 1980 Republicans had rebuilt their number of seats to thirteen, but the redistricting of 1982 again pushed them back down to ten. Republicans have not forgotten this experience and will surely use the process to solidify their legislative control for the near future.

But Republicans cannot be sanguine about Florida's quixotic voters, especially in light of the 2000 presidential election. Although the party has enjoyed popular support, Republicans must continue to attract substantial numbers of Democrats and independents to capture statewide races. That may be difficult in the wake of the 2000 election. Moreover, Floridians are divided ideologically, demographically, ethnically, and racially. No party can be confident in such a political environment—especially because enormous numbers of Baby Boomers soon will retire to Florida and their political affiliation is uncertain.

Among Florida's crossover voters are the crackers. In analyzing Florida politics, it is best to think of crackers as a distinct partisan grouping. From the Reconstruction era through the 1930s they were so loyal to the Democratic Party that they were called "yellow dog Democrats." In other words, they would vote for a Democrat, even if the candidate resembled an unattractive yellow dog. Cracker ties to the Democratic Party at the national level began to weaken, however, because of political differences with Franklin Roosevelt's New Deal programs and the party's appeal to black voters. By 1948 white southern Democrats had become so enraged by the policies of the national party that Strom Thurmond, then governor of South Carolina, launched a third-party candidacy for the presidency as a "Dixiecrat." Not two decades later, when Democratic majorities in the U.S. House and Senate approved the Civil Rights Act of 1964 and the Voting Rights Act of 1965, Democrats in the South further distanced themselves from the national party. In the 1960s crackers also began voting Republican in many statewide elections. Today the term *southern Democrat* is passé because the conflict about civil rights has subsided, but cracker Democrats are still viewed as distinct from other members of the party. They are now occasionally referred to as "blue dog Democrats," because they will often vote Republican (and blue is the GOP's color).

Efforts to court the cracker vote have gradually declined since 1968 as their numbers have waned, but in both the 1994 gubernatorial election and the disputed 2000 presidential election, cracker Democrats played a crucial role in the outcomes. In the 1994 gubernatorial campaign, incumbent governor Lawton Chiles saw white, rural, conservative Democrats as the key to victory in his race against Jeb Bush. In the first debate with Bush, Chiles announced that he "spoke cracker," and in the last debate he referred to himself as an "old he-coon."[1] These comments carried little weight and made little sense in the retirement communities of Broward County or among the professors at Florida State University or the University of Florida. But Governor Chiles knew how close this race would be and that he needed the native rural vote to defeat Bush. When he won, Chiles's margin of victory was the second narrowest for a statewide race in Florida history.

Dixiecrats, Republicans, Democrats, and the 1998 Election

Republicans have been hoping to turn Florida into a solidly Republican state by persuading conservative Democrats to become full-time Republicans, but so far they have not succeeded. Although Jeb Bush and his lieutenant governor, Frank Brogan, won a decisive victory over Democrats Buddy MacKay and Rick Dantzler in the 1998 gubernatorial contest, their victory did not force the political realignment that GOP leaders had sought. Most of the largest, historically Democratic counties in fact voted Democratic, and the historically Republican counties voted Republican. The Dixiecrat counties, while tilting for Bush, were nevertheless more evenly divided than other areas of the state. Bush and Brogan won by a large margin, not because they had succeeded in forging a new voter coalition but because many Democratic voters failed to vote.

The vote totals for the gubernatorial tickets in 1994 and 1998 reveal the results of this low turnout for Democrats. Bush gained few votes between the two elections. In 1994 he received a little more than 2 million votes, and in 1998 he received 2.1 million. These numbers are even more significant because state Republicans added more than 500,000 registered voters between 1994 and 1998. By comparison, in 1994 Chiles-MacKay drew 2.1 million votes, but in 1998 MacKay-Dantzler received only 1.77 million votes, 364,000 fewer, even though the number of registered Democrats had increased by 400,000. MacKay and Dantzler simply failed to interest the party's electoral base in their campaign.

So, despite substantial gains made by Republicans since the mid-1980s, the two major parties still appear closely matched, and subsequent events could tip the political scales one way or the other. Indeed, the Baby Boomers and Hispanic voters could well play the decisive role in determining the outcome of this political rivalry.

The key question with respect to the Cuban-American vote in Florida is whether this group will remain committed to the Republican Party. Most Cuban immigrants have been Republicans because they regard the party's anticommunist views as much more in line with their concerns about their native land and their opposition to Fidel Castro. Many third-generation Cuban Americans, however, are much less dogmatic in their political views and in their anticommunism. Should Castro die or fall from power, the commitment of Cuban Americans to the Republican Party is likely to diminish, perhaps dramatically.

Similarly, Baby Boomers are more progressive in their political views than their parents, so traditional appeals to retirees may not resonate as well with Boomers. Certainly, their political values are different from those of their parents, but how this difference will affect the two political parties in Florida is not certain. It does seem clear, however, that both parties will have to alter their appeals to capture the vote of Boomers, and those changes will certainly affect political discourse in Florida and perhaps the political leadership.

The 2000 Presidential Election and Florida's Political Future

The controversy surrounding the 2000 presidential election in Florida complicated Republican ambitions and offered an intriguing glimpse into Florida's political future. The election dispute involved all the elements we have mentioned: seniors, African Americans, Hispanics, and rural voters; the legislative and executive branches of government; and a sharply divided electorate. At times the controversy surrounding the election was dizzying, as first one agency of government made a decision and then another countermanded it. Partisanship was pervasive, and old-boy political informality in some rural counties resulted in election irregularities and illegalities. The controversy was a strange brew of antiquated procedures, intense electoral divisions, biased public officials, massive media attention, and unusually high stakes.

At the outset of the presidential campaign, political experts widely predicted that Jeb Bush would deliver the state for his brother, George W. What they underestimated was Democratic strength in Florida, and they overlooked the state's continually changing demographics. The mobilization of African-American voters and seniors in condominiums in southeast Florida, as well as non-Cuban Hispanic voters (especially Puerto Ricans, who have traditionally voted Democratic), gave Al Gore a legitimate chance in the state. Gore sought black and minority votes by railing against Jeb Bush, and indirectly his brother, for the executive order that banned further use of affirmative action in Florida. African-American voters nearly carried Jacksonville for Gore and might have succeeded in doing so if many of their votes had not been invalidated. Puerto Ricans helped push Orange County into the Democratic column for the first time in a presidential contest since 1948.

Both Gore and Bush campaigned heavily to get the votes of blue dog Democrats, because, as they say in rural Florida, they don't necessarily go home from the dance with the one who brung 'em. Gore came to Tallahassee early—in March—and surrounded himself with the likes of Rhea Chiles and Mary Call Darby Collins, widows of two of the political giants of twentieth-century Florida. Because the husbands of both women had done well with the blue dog Democrats, Gore hoped their support would help him with these voters.

For his part, Bush found himself forced to visit the blue dog counties in the Panhandle and North-Central Florida late in the campaign, when he would have preferred to be elsewhere, but he could not afford to lose Florida. During the last week of the campaign the entire Bush family showed up in rural North Florida. In the end, Bush did well with the blue dog vote, but that did not guarantee his victory.

Florida was ill prepared for the controversy surrounding the presidential election of 2000, despite election law reforms in 1989 and 1999. The reforms had failed to develop a satisfactory method for recounting disputed ballots, and these ballots and how to tabulate them became the crux of the 2000 election.

Although Florida's county election supervisors reported to the secretary of state that George W. Bush had carried Florida by 1,784 votes, the election remained in doubt because election officials had discarded 185,000 ballots as unreadable for one reason or another. Clouding the entire process were the chads that had not been punched through when voters cast their ballots using punched cards.[2] The proportion of votes miscast in the counties with the punched card system was roughly three times the proportion of miscast votes in counties using optical scanners. Of the fifty-one precincts in which more than 20 percent of ballots were discarded, forty-five (88 percent) used punched cards. Of the 336 precincts in which more than 10 percent were rejected, 277 (78 percent) used punched cards.[3]

Complicating the results further, many senior voters were confused by the butterfly ballot that Palm Beach County used. Normally, ballots in a punched card system like that county's are laid out with the candidates' names listed alphabetically and a series of holes to the left of the candidates' names. But the butterfly ballot listed candidates on both the left and right sides of the ballot, and voters were supposed to punch a hole in the center. An added difficulty in some precincts in Palm Beach County was that the holes did not line up with the candidates' names on some ballots. As a result, seniors gave Patrick Buchanan an unusually high number of votes in the county (about 3,500) relative to the number of voters registered with the Reform Party (about 330), and 1,900 voters in the county had punched more than one hole in the presidential column. Had these votes been properly cast for Gore, as these seniors seem to have intended, Gore would have won Florida.[4]

During the recounting the twenty-five counties with the punched card system used machines to conduct the recount. By the end of this process Bush's lead had dropped by half, to a little more than 900 votes. Most of the increase for Gore occurred because sending punched cards through the vote-tabulating machines causes impartially punched chads to break free; as a result, votes previously obscured became visible, and many entered the Gore column.

From the outset the recount became mired in intense partisanship as each side sought victory for its presidential candidate, and Florida's process for selecting election officials heightened the claims of partisanship by both sides. Supporters for both candidates, for example, complained that local election supervisors who had run for office as Democrats or Republicans were biased. But Democrats saved their greatest fury for Secretary of State Katherine Harris, who was a Republican and cochair of the Bush campaign in Florida. Adding to these complaints was the fact that sitting on the State Elections Commission, which certifies the accuracy of all statewide elections, were the secretary of state, the governor, and the director of the division of elections.

While the outcome may have had much to do with errors made by voters and poorly designed ballots, partisan politics took center stage. Three of the state's highest-ranking public officials—Harris, Governor Bush, and Attorney General Bob Butterworth—had direct ties to one of the candidates in the dispute. Jeb Bush and Harris had cochaired George W.'s Florida campaign, and Butterworth chaired the Florida campaign for Gore. Just on its face, Florida's election process appeared vulnerable to partisan intrigues. Moreover, a series of articles published in the *Washington Post* a few weeks after the election controversy revealed that some actions and decisions of Bush, Harris, and Butterworth were coordinated directly or indirectly with the strategies of the candidates' respective legal teams.[5]

Was this election a wake-up call for Florida in the twenty-first century? While the precise events of the disputed 2000 presidential election are unlikely to be repeated, the intensity and closeness of the election have appeared in two other recent state contests: the 1988 U.S. Senate race, when Republican Connie Mack defeated Democrat Buddy Mac-Kay, and the 1994 gubernatorial election, when Jeb Bush lost to Lawton Chiles. Although 4 million voters cast ballots in the Mack-MacKay election, it was decided by 32,000 votes, and MacKay had the edge until the absentee ballots were counted. At the time this was the closest statewide election in Florida. In 1994 Chiles beat Jeb Bush by a margin of only 65,000 votes.

Democrats in Florida came away from the 2000 election extremely frustrated not only because Gore lost but also because many of their votes were discarded. The two political groups that were angriest and that felt most harmed by polling errors were African Americans and seniors. The county with the highest error rate (12 percent of all votes cast) was Gadsden, the only black-majority county in Florida; the county where voter confusion was most prevalent was Palm Beach, with its substantial senior population.

Concerns about the 2000 presidential election are likely to influence Florida government and politics for the foreseeable future, and the election process is likely to remain a flash point in state politics, because demographic trends promise to keep either party from seizing the majority. With its diverse populations Florida faces the persistent threat of political alienation and anger about election issues. All the major constituent groups in the state—seniors, African Americans, and Hispanics—felt their votes were not fairly or fully counted. As all these groups continue to grow, the potential for additional close statewide elections and the attendant frustration appears to be great.

Florida's Environmental, Racial, and Urban Challenges

With these ongoing changes in Florida's population and politics, the state's ability to address its environmental and urban problems should actually improve. Aiding this transition has been the decline in influence of the state's rural voters because they are no longer in a position to block efforts to control urban sprawl, provide urban services and facilities, or broaden the scope and level of taxation to accommodate the demands of the state's population growth.

The principal cause of most of these problems remains the state's sprawling pattern of urbanization, which is likely to persist and even accelerate during the twenty-first century. Florida's major challenges fall into four categories: environmental, social, political, and economic. Table 8 shows the basic problems within each category.

Table 8. Problems caused by Florida's growth

Environmental problems
    Water pollution
    Water shortages
    Destruction of wildlife and wildlife habitats
    Degradation of intact ecosystems
Social problems
    Urban blight
    Racially segregated schools
Political problems
    Recurring fiscal crises
    Inadequate public facilities and services
Economic problems
    Loss of prime agricultural lands
    Shift toward low-wage jobs in service sector

Table 9. Growth in Florida's major urban areas, 1940–2000

Rank	Metro area	1940 pop.	2000 pop.	% change
2	Sarasota-Bradenton	42,204	589,959	1297.8
3	West Palm Beach	79,989	1,131,184	1314.1
5	Miami–Ft. Lauderdale	307,533	3,876,380	1160.4
6	Orlando	129,752	1,664,561	1182.8
10	Tampa–St. Petersburg	291,622	2,395,997	721.6

Source: Bureau of Economic and Business Research, Florida Statistical Abstract, 2001, 35th ed., 51.

Environmental Degradation

The state's massive population growth since 1945 has led to the development of many large urban centers that are surrounded by miles and miles of moderate-density housing interspersed with strip shopping centers, office parks, and regional malls. Although the state's population growth is expected to slow down for the near future, Florida's largest urban communities will experience significant growth, with cities in the southern part of the state continuing to bear the brunt of much of the population expansion. The disproportionate nature of this growth in the central and southern areas of the state poses the biggest challenge to Florida. These are the areas in which most growth took place between 1945 and 2000 and the ones with the most serious water and environmental problems.

Tables 9 and 10 show the rate of growth in the state's major urban areas between 1940 and 2000 and project growth for these communities from 2000 to 2020. In the fifty years after World War II, five of the ten fastest-growing cities in the nation were in Florida, and four of the five were in the central and southern parts of the state where the water resources and the environment are especially fragile.

Four of these regions will continue to be the fastest growing in Florida, with the West Palm Beach–Boca Raton area expected to be the seventh fastest in the United States. The growth will begin to shift farther north, and areas like Jacksonville and nearby counties will see rapid growth. Although the growth rates for these cities are likely to be lower than they were from 1950 to 2000, they will still significantly affect the quality of life and the demand for drinking water, especially

Table 10. Growth projected for Florida's major urban areas, 2000–2020

Rank	Metro area	% change	2000	2020 (proj.)
5	Orlando	+56.29%	1,644,561	2,173,267
7	West Palm Beach–Boca Raton	+54.73%	1,131,184	1,504,081
17	Tampa–St. Petersburg	+35.90%	2,395,997	2,963,304
22	Jacksonville	+32.27%	1,100,491	1,295,018
29	Miami–Ft. Lauderdale	+23.20%	3,876,380	4,242,245

in the regions of West Palm Beach–Boca Raton, Tampa–St. Petersburg, and Miami–Fort Lauderdale. Unless these metropolises develop cooperative arrangements, or alternatives such as saltwater conversion plants, Florida will almost certainly experience major conflicts between the water-rich central and northern regions of the state and the water-starved southern regions. Such conflicts would make the water wars between Pasco and Pinellas counties in the mid-1990s look like an Orlando tourist attraction. As Pinellas ran short of potable water, it contracted with Pasco for access to its water. When the water supply in Pasco declined dramatically, county leaders reneged on the contract, and Pinellas took them to court. A great deal of name-calling followed, and drinking water suddenly became a critical issue for Florida.

Although the state's dramatic population growth may well slow down in the future, *growth* remains a relative term in Florida. By any measure, urban growth will be substantial, and it will compound the state's water, environmental, and social issues.

Environmental degradation in Florida has occurred as this urban growth has spread into the state's many marshes and wetlands. When the latter are drained or when roads are run through them, the environmental damage is extensive, far greater than what first meets the eye. Here is a brief rundown of Florida's most serious environmental problems.

• *Destruction of the natural system of water supply.* The southern region of the state is dependent for its water supply on underground aquifers, which are replenished by shallow surface waters as they flow down the center of the state into the Everglades. As population growth has occurred in the coastal areas, and as fringe areas of the Everglades have been drained and developed, the water supply in the southern part of the state has been depleted.

- *Water pollution.* Urbanization brings with it what is sometimes called "nonsource pollution." Oil dripped from cars, old car batteries thrown into canals, waste flowing from septic tanks, and other pollutants associated with urbanization seep into the underground water supply. Unlike industrial water pollution, which can be tracked to its source and prohibited, nonsource pollution has no single point of origin and is therefore almost impossible to control in high-growth areas.

- *Destruction of wildlife species and habitats.* Florida's state animal, the Florida panther, has been driven almost to extinction; only thirty panthers are believed to remain in the wild today. Most have been killed while crossing highways that run through their habitats. Also threatened are manatees and numerous bird species that live on fish and other wildlife in the state's wetlands. Many bird species are at risk because drainage of wetlands is destroying the habitat of their food supply.

- *Degradation of intact ecosystems, notably lakes and bays.* Some of the state's largest lakes and wetlands have been destroyed by wastes washed into them from nearby agriculture and by water runoff from urban areas. Rainwater from farms sends fertilizer into the lakes, causing algae blooms, which deprive the lakes of oxygen, ultimately killing their fish. Similarly, bays in metropolitan areas are polluted by urban runoff and by excessive amounts of freshwater flowing into them from drainage systems built to prevent inland flooding.[6]

Racial Segregation and the Blight Belt

In the late 1960s, when most of Florida was still agricultural and the coastal towns were small, the main north-south highways on each coast—U.S. 41 on the west and U.S. 1 on the east—served as informal borders with obvious racial and social implications. With the exception of the largest and oldest cities, the wealthiest residents and virtually all the urban whites lived on the coastal side of the highway, while African

Americans lived farther inland. The north-south highways were the "Main Streets" around which the small rural towns developed. The downtowns—if they could be called that—had concentrations of shops and restaurants, motels, and a variety of businesses to serve both the tourists and local residents.

As population grew and urban sprawl spread inland, roads and malls were constructed, pulling most of the shoppers from the old coastal downtowns. The new suburbs spread inland to the edge of the Everglades, leaving the old urban centers and their indigenous African-American populations behind. Today U.S. 41 from Tampa south through Naples and U.S. 1 from south of Jacksonville to Miami weave through a belt of urban blight that parallels most of Florida's coastline. On the east coast Jacksonville, St. Augustine, and Daytona Beach were well established before highways began dividing communities. In the other communities, however, virtually the same pattern exists all along the west side of U.S. 1: warehouses, new commercial development, and upscale residential areas are punctuated approximately every five miles by poor, predominantly African-American neighborhoods. In a few instances, such as Pearl City in Boca Raton, minority residential areas have remained stable and well kept, but more often they are ignored by local officials and are run down and crime-ridden. Civic leaders seem concerned only when the properties on which these black neighborhoods are located suddenly became valuable, as occurred in Cocoa, Florida. There, after years of neglecting the black neighborhood near U.S. 1, city officials in the early 1990s became interested in it as a location for an upscale boating marina to attract tourists and wealthy residents. Only the threat of a lawsuit by the Legal Defense Fund of the NAACP blocked efforts to condemn the neighborhood. Despite this small victory, pockets of African-American poverty remain evident in almost every older town along Florida's east and southwest coasts.

Florida's blight belt is both a legacy of segregation and the result of a changing economy that left the old, the ill, and the insufficiently educated trapped in a narrow strip of land between the old Florida and the new as mechanization and urban growth replaced nearby agricultural and citrus jobs. Many African Americans took advantage of the new opportunities, but many could not.

Urban sprawl and school desegregation have further exacerbated Florida's racial environment. Throughout Central and South Florida the vast majority of white newcomers have populated pristine inland suburbs far from the old coastal cities. African Americans, meanwhile, have largely remained in the blight belt along the coastal highways. When the federal courts ordered the desegregation of Florida's public schools, urban school districts opted to build schools equidistant between the coastal cities and the expanding white inland suburbs and then bused children to them from both directions. This process has frequently worsened the problems of the blight belt by eliminating the integrated schools in the coastal cities, particularly the neighborhood schools in black communities that also constituted an important center of black community life. Although this policy minimized travel time for the students, the closing of coastal schools also further promoted "white flight" to the suburban areas.

Inadequate Public Facilities and Services—The "See a Cow" Rule

Another serious political problem facing Florida, and resulting in part from urban sprawl, has been an endemic fiscal crisis. Growth has placed a heavy burden on state and local governments to provide roads, water and sewer systems, schools, and other public facilities. But Florida's tax structure is such that state leaders cannot pay for these facilities without constantly going back to voters for increases in the tax rate. And Floridians have typically rejected such requests in the past two decades.

In principle, state and local governments can raise tax revenues in three ways. They can tax property, they can tax income, and they can tax transactions or sales. In the 1930s the state chose to focus on transactions as its source of revenue, and an old Florida saying reflected the reason why: "Don't tax you, don't tax me, tax the guys behind the tree." The folks behind the tree are the tourists. Florida's tax structure is deliberately aimed at tourists and away from permanent residents. As a consequence, it is slanted heavily toward taxes on transactions. Florida remains one of only eight states in the nation without an individual income tax, and property taxes are restricted by both a thirty-mill cap (ten mills for any single taxing unit) and a $25,000 homestead exemption.[7] By contrast, the state sales tax is quite high at 6 percent; only eight other states have a sales tax equal to or higher than Florida's.

Florida also restricts taxes in several other ways. Agricultural land, for example, is taxed at a low rate, even when it is in or near urban areas. This policy is a throwback to an earlier agricultural era and reflects the influence of rural voters on state policy. Vacant land in Florida's suburban areas typically has a cow or two on it to ensure that it is taxed as agricultural land. Florida's "see a cow" rule remains a standing joke in the state. According to the rule, if a cow is grazing on the land, it must be a farm and thus should receive the low (agricultural) tax rate. Another constraint on taxing state residents is the Save Our Homes Amendment, which, like Proposition 13 in California, limits increases in assessed valuation while homeowners retain their property. As defined, the assessed value can increase no more than the rate of inflation or 3 percent, whichever is less. In addition to these restrictions, Floridians passed a constitutional amendment in 1998 authorizing a second $25,000 homestead exemption for retirees with low incomes.

Florida's decision to avoid taxing its residents and to rely instead on sales taxes may have been appropriate when Florida was a predominantly poor rural state in the first half of the twentieth century. With relatively few residents during this period and an expanding number of rather well-to-do tourists, Florida was able to finance most of its state and local government needs through the so-called tourist tax. State leaders also used low taxes as a device to attract new residents and new businesses to Florida.

In this rapidly growing urban state of the twenty-first century, however, dependence on a sales tax makes little sense and has inevitably led to numerous shortfalls in revenue since the early 1970s. Although the state's population has exploded, sales tax revenues have not kept pace with newcomers' needs for public facilities. Per capita revenues from a 6 percent sales tax amount to approximately $400 per person per year (man, woman, and child), whether the state has one million residents or 20 million. As costs escalate rapidly in urban growth areas, however, facilities and services are much more expensive than in rural areas.

Wastewater treatment plants cost more than septic tanks, SWAT teams and vice squads cost more than road patrols, and highways with overpasses and traffic signals cost more than two-lane roads with stop signs. With costs thus rising faster than revenues, urban communities have frequently found themselves unable to pay the bill for growth.

These cities have avoided financial bankruptcy by cutting back on services and facilities even while growth has continued. The result has been a declining quality of life in many of the state's larger communities. The basic requirements of urban life—schools, roads, water and sewer lines—remain available, but residents are forced to live with heavy traffic, crowded beaches, polluted water, and "temporary" school buildings that are, for all practical purposes, permanent.

Growth Management and Its Failures in Florida

Florida's political leaders have developed a combination of policies to address massive growth, urban sprawl, and the tax mentality of its citizens. Referred to as "growth management," state laws have created a system of state, regional, and local land-use planning, regulation, and environmental protection. Growth management seeks to ensure that urbanization is orderly and that public facilities and services keep abreast of development. The laws use a variety of mechanisms to require state, regional, and local units of government to plan for growth, to adjust their plans and actions to one another, and to either raise taxes or restrict development as necessary to keep development and public facilities in harmony.

In the 1960s most parts of the state created regional planning bodies, but the idea of requiring government to plan for growth had not yet taken hold. Indeed, the state legislature, still controlled by the North Florida delegation, failed until the end of the decade to enact legislation that would merely *allow* local governments to develop and implement growth plans.

Only after reapportionment of the state legislature in 1969 did Florida begin to deal comprehensively with its massive population growth. It put in place a combination of land development regulations that attempted to restrict development. This legislation was effective in protecting particularly sensitive environmental resources and in making large-scale development environmentally friendlier, but it had virtually no effect on the state's untoward pattern of urbanization. A second wave of legislation in the mid-1980s produced similar results. The legislation began as an attempt to contain urban sprawl, but powerful political opposition to its potential restrictions on property rights emerged and defeated many of its key features. A third wave of growth management reforms, launched in the 1990s, also failed because of a political backlash from developers.

Today Florida has one of the most complicated and far-reaching systems of growth management and environmental protection in the nation, but the system's complexity and breadth have not brought success. Although it has been overhauled three times and fine-tuned many more times than that, the policy framework has repeatedly failed to achieve its intended results. The main weakness of Florida's approach has been its inability to prevent the intrusion of urbanization into the state's most sensitive ecosystems. As a result, Florida has beautiful subdivisions with manicured landscaping, while the Everglades faces one crisis after another, canals along the coast of southwest Florida and in the Keys are polluted, and lakes in several counties are drying up.

Efforts to reform Florida's tax structure by linking it to this growth management framework have been disappointing. The hope of tax reformers, especially in the mid-1980s, was that, if developers were required to provide adequate public facilities, pressure would build on the business community to broaden Florida's tax base. Few supporters of tax reform expected Florida to adopt an income tax, but they thought that exemptions to the state's sales tax would be trimmed. Their efforts went for naught, however. Despite several tries, both Democrats and Republicans balked at tax reform.

The Internet, however, threatens to destabilize state revenues and force state political leaders to pursue tax changes. More and more Floridians are ordering goods and services through the Internet, and these purchases are not subject to the state's sales tax. Economists anticipate that Florida's tax revenues soon will be inadequate to support its basic infrastructure as the Internet's reach expands and on-line purchases accelerate.

The Baby Boomer Retirement Wave

About to complicate Florida's growth management and its financial future is a huge wave of retirees. It may come as a surprise to many that the Baby Boomers will exacerbate the state's environmental and urban problems, but there are a number of reasons to expect that they will.

Retirement and Sprawl

First, Baby Boomers will place added pressure on the environment because, like other retirees before them, they will be able to choose a residential location without concern for their place of employment. Retirees have frequently opted to live on the fringes of the major employment centers, such as Tampa, so they can remain close to urban amenities while escaping the noise, urban traffic, higher city taxes, crime, and overcrowding. Because retirees will dominate Florida's population growth for the next twenty-five years, they will significantly influence settlement patterns in many counties.

Many counties will experience a four-stage process of urbanization as retirees settle in them. In the first stage retirees move into rural areas that are adjacent to cities with good urban services. Then young people arrive behind the retirees to provide essential services for them. In the third stage these communities expand to offer goods and services to the young adults. In the last stage the retirees begin to move into the next county or an unincorporated area as the community becomes too congested for them.

The southeast coast of Florida has already witnessed these retiree-driven settlement patterns. In the 1980s Broward County became a large retirement center as seniors moved away from a deteriorating Miami Beach. Developers built huge condominium buildings and complexes on the coast and inland on what had been agricultural land and citrus groves. Many younger people then moved in to provide seniors with various services, and new businesses emerged to serve young adults. However, in the early 1990s the retirement population in Broward started to abandon the area for Palm Beach County and communities farther north to avoid crime, traffic, and new immigrants.

This sprawling pattern of urbanization is an environmental and social nightmare. It paves over water recharge areas, pollutes nearby lakes and rivers, disrupts the state's large water-dependent ecosystems, and puts wildlife in the path of automobiles and boats. As urbanization pushes north along Florida's southeast and southwest coasts and farther inland, the economies of the old coastal cities deteriorate and so do the poor communities that depended on these economies. Coastal schools are closed as new schools are built inland to accommodate population growth, further disrupting poor neighborhoods. The results are urban blight and environmental problems as the population spreads over sensitive lands, and saltwater intrudes into coastal wellfields.

Retirees and Fiscal Stress on Florida

Baby Boomers will compound Florida's environmental and urban problems in yet another way when they become frail and require public services and facilities. Retirees have generally been an economic boon to Florida because they have lived in the state during the first ten to fifteen years of their retirement, when they have generally been healthy. Most moved to Florida when they were sixty to sixty-five years old, then moved back to their home states to be near their children when they reached their mid-seventies or as they became frail. Thus they typically lived in Florida when they were healthy, able to spend money on a range of goods and services, and needed few health-care and human services.

However, this pattern has been changing rapidly in recent years as more and more retirees opt to become permanent residents of the state. In addition, an increasing number of the children of retirees now live in Florida and not elsewhere. With their children here many retirees are choosing to remain in the state well beyond their seventy-fifth year.

As more seniors stay in the state into their eighties and nineties and are joined by Baby Boomers, they will place extraordinary demands on state services and facilities. Florida has already begun to witness the fiscal costs associated with the aging of its population. In 1979 the state's Medicaid expenses came to less than $200 million (the program picks up some medical expenses for the poor, including nursing home care for the indigent elderly); by 1997 the bill had reached $1.3 billion. In the same year more than half the state's Medicaid budget went for nursing home care for senior citizens. In 2001 the legislature found itself with a $1 billion Medicaid bill that it had assumed would be closer to $400 million.[8] These soaring Medicaid costs, however, will no doubt pale next to those generated by a very large number of Baby Boomers. Florida also must face the possibility that state revenues could grow more slowly, because many seniors will be able to take advantage of both the Save Our Homes Amendment and the second homestead exemption to reduce their taxes. The fiscal picture for the state is problematic, yet there has been literally no public discussion of this likely scenario or how the state might prepare for it.

Seniors and the Service Economy

The growth in the Baby Boomer population also threatens to disrupt Florida's low-wage economy. Many jobs in industries that serve senior citizens require few skills, pay low wages, and provide little opportunity for advancement. To be sure, some retirement-related industries are at the top of the economic pyramid, particularly medical services and the health-care industry. But most businesses that cater to retirees are in the less lucrative service sector, from retail services to congregate facilities to food services. Florida already has numerous low-wage, service-related jobs in the tourist sector, and the consensus among business and policy leaders is that it needs more skilled, high-technology jobs, not more service positions. Union leaders also contend that Florida's right-to-work law keeps wages low, and there is evidence to support their contention.

The Politics of the Twenty-first Century

To state the obvious, Baby Boomers will stimulate major changes in Florida's political environment. Both parties have already begun soliciting their votes by focusing on programs that address their needs. Florida will see more of this in the coming years. Despite its current advantages, the Republican Party has to be concerned about the increasing numbers of retirees and their anger about the 2000 election. Moreover, many of those who will soon retire are at odds with the party's position on environmental, gender, and racial issues. How both parties adjust their political platforms to address concerns of this generation of retirees will likely determine which party will control the state in the twenty-first century.

Demographically and politically, Florida will enter a new period in its history when the Baby Boomers retire. Certainly, if any generation could embrace the need for change and assume political leadership and responsibility, it is this generation, which supported an end to racial segregation, embraced equal opportunity for women, launched the environmental movement, ended the cold war, and helped digitize the world's economy.

But when they retire to Florida, Baby Boomers will encounter a government and a culture that historically have been quite conservative, regardless of the party in power. Whether cracker or Cuban, midwesterner or northeasterner, Floridians have consistently opposed more government. It appears quite likely that Baby Boomers will challenge that political philosophy as they seek ways to address their needs in health care, housing, work, and transportation. The rest of the nation will watch the confrontation in Florida with great interest, because other states are likely to face a similar scenario.

What, then, will the policy agenda for Florida look like in the twenty-first century? In chapter 6 we look at issues that have become prominent in recent years, how they and other policy agendas will unfold in the new century, and the ways in which the transition to the future can occur more quickly and smoothly in Florida.

LeRoy
COLLINS

Farris
BRYANT

Fuller
WARREN

SUMTER L.
LOWRY

THE POLITICAL LAWYER CANDIDATES

A VOTE FOR ANY ONE OF THESE . . .
IS A VOTE FOR

EXPERIENCED BUSINESSMAN

A VOTE FOR LOWRY IS
A VOTE TO KEEP

RACE MIXING!

WHITE SCHOOLS WHITE

PROTECT

- THE SOVEREIGNTY OF THE STATE OF FLORIDA
- THE OPPORTUNITY AND SOUND DEVELOPMENT OF FLORIDA
- YOUR SOCIAL AND ECONOMIC WELFARE
- YOUR CHILDREN'S FUTURE

Vote for - **SUMTER L. LOWRY** *and* -

KEEP WHITE SCHOOLS WHITE

LOWRY for GOVERNOR
CAMPAIGN COMMITTEE
304 O'REILLY BUILDING
JACKSONVILLE 2, FLORIDA

BULK RATE
U. S. POSTAGE
PAID
Jacksonville, Florida
Permit No. 2219

Rural Box Holder
Local

SUMTER L. LOWRY
CANDIDATE FOR GOVERNOR
THE TRUTH ABOUT THE FOUR MAJOR CANDIDATES **FOR GOVERNOR**

In the state Democratic primary of 1956, three candidates vied with Governor LeRoy Collins for the governorship. The *Brown* decision of 1954 ordering school desegregation had become a major issue in the state by 1956. The three candidates challenging Collins used the race issue, and the most extreme of them was Sumter Lowry. Collins won and ensured that Florida would pursue a moderate course of action in the battle over desegregation. Courtesy P. K. Yonge Library of Florida History.

In the 1960s, civil rights activists, led by the Reverend Martin Luther King, Jr., conducted demonstrations against tourist sites in Florida to put economic pressure on the state government to agree to integration. In this photograph, the demonstrations took place on the beach in Ft. Lauderdale to protest segregation and discrimination

Although Florida modernized rapidly after World War II, its racial environment remained a major obstacle to progress. Protests in the 1960s by young blacks and whites, such as this one in Tallahassee, helped turn the tide against segregation, enabling Florida to get beyond the legacy of racism.

During the postwar period, black citizens sought an end to segregation in Florida by reminding residents of their sacrifices for the nation during the war. Harry Moore, president of the Florida branch of the NAACP, led this effort and found himself physically threatened by white militants. On Christmas night 1951, Moore and his wife, Harriet, were killed when a bomb was placed beneath their home.

The campaign to desegregate Florida and to further the cause of freedom did not stop with the death of the Moores. A Freedom Bus arrived in Tallahassee to rally black Floridians behind the desegregation effort.

Governor Reubin Askew introducing newly appointed Secretary of State Jesse McCrary in 1978. McCrary was the first African American to serve in the Florida cabinet in the twentieth century.

Protests against the draft, which spread across the nation during the Vietnam War and after, also occurred on college campuses on the eve of the conflict with Iraq. Students opposed the war and their involvement in it with signs reading "Hell No, We Won't Go."

In the 1980s, women, men, and children rallied on behalf of the Equal Rights Amendment and urged Floridians to support the amendment to the Constitution. A strong counter-demonstration led by a group of women in Florida helped to mobilize support against the ERA movement on the grounds that the amendment would undermine family, religion, and society.

Bob Graham worked at 100 different jobs during his gubernatorial campaign in 1976 to win the support of "everyday" voters. Once in office, he continued this practice, believing that it kept him in touch with the state's citizens and aware of their needs and concerns. He also continued it when he became a U.S. senator. Here he worked in 1979 alongside Willie Lee Rasberry and Samuel DeLoach unloading sod grass.

Governor Lawton Chiles and Lieutenant Governor Buddy MacKay were joined by children and parents in launching their 1994 campaign. Chiles narrowly defeated Republican Jeb Bush in the closest gubernatorial contest of the twentieth century. Their campaign featured the educational and social needs of Florida's children, in which the state showed poorly in several categories of national rankings of children's services.

Left: Few photographs capture the emergence of modern Florida better than this one: The space shuttle, sitting atop a Boeing 747, is flown to Cape Canaveral over the state capitol in Tallahassee.

Below: Florida also captured the nation's imagination as the launch site for space exploration. In 1981, the United States launched the space shuttle Columbia, the first shuttle launch and the prototype of the spaceship that would be reused throughout the late twentieth century and into the twenty-first for exploration and construction of the space station.

chapter 6

The Political Challenges
of the Twenty-first Century

What can Florida's leaders do to prepare for the demands that will inevitably accompany the increasing age and diversity of the population? There are no easy answers, but in this concluding chapter we offer a few thoughts about these issues and about a process for identifying solutions. In our view Florida faces a number of daunting challenges that can be addressed only by skilled leaders who will not shy away from controversy and by engaged citizens who will not be readily manipulated by partisan propaganda. Most well-informed Floridians agree that the state will need to modernize its tax structure, expand its programs for the elderly, improve its educational system, increase awareness about the value of diversity, assume greater responsibility for its environment and water resources, and make other public policy adjustments to address the challenges of the new millennium. However, we believe it is equally important to decide what must be done and *how* to do it. In our view the greatest challenge for Florida in the coming decades will be developing the political will to respond to mounting environmental, economic, and social pressures. Florida is so large geographically, so diverse culturally and regionally, so affected by the political activism of seniors, and so buffeted by migration and immigration patterns that its citizens do not readily find consensus on issues, even when they widely acknowledge the need for action. Thus the task for policy makers is not simply to devise sound solutions to the state's problems but to educate and mobilize the citizenry to understand and support the solutions.

This by itself is an intimidating task, but complicating it are the forces of reaction that historically have emerged in Florida whenever bold action is called for. At the risk of oversimplification, the modern history of Florida has been a protracted and painful process of moving the state away from its race-conscious southern heritage into the national mainstream. Even today Florida's political institutions have features that were put in place long ago to maintain the needs of a different society and of white dominance.

A second major factor complicating Florida's response to these challenges is that several policies must not merely be adjusted but reversed. Ironically, some attitudes and policies developed in the twentieth century to help modernize Florida now threaten its environment, economy, and quality of life. To stimulate population growth and economic development, state and local governments helped drain land for farming and construction, limited the state's authority to tax, welcomed low-wage agricultural labor from other nations, sold public lands to pay for public works, permitted the construction of septic tanks without regard for the environment, and opened their arms to all who wanted to live in the state. Reversing these policies has already begun with the adoption of a corporate income tax, growth management laws, water use permits, and the planned restoration of the Everglades. But the state needs to make still more major policy reversals, including its public philosophy of growth at any cost.

Preparing for the future runs counter to one of the maxims heard most often in Florida: "If it ain't broke, don't fix it." Any new policies that try to address the needs of Florida's aging and diverse populations must account for this laissez-faire attitude and recognize, as a consequence, that building a substantial public constituency for reform is difficult.

Guiding the Old Florida into a New Era

To chart a path to the present let us take a last look at the past to see how earlier leaders overcame political obstacles as seemingly intractable as those that the state faces today. Undoubtedly, Florida's biggest challenge during the twentieth century was confronting racial segregation. Desegregation occurred with less conflict in Florida than in any other southern state, with the possible exception of North Carolina. Governors LeRoy Collins and Reubin Askew guided Florida through this era with extraordinary skill, while states like Alabama, Georgia, Mississippi, South Carolina, and Arkansas experienced the worst excesses of white racism and gubernatorial leadership that catered to it. Although Floridians opposed desegregation as much as their southern neighbors, they avoided much of the violence and anguish of this era because of the leadership of Collins and Askew.

How did Collins and Askew manage this in a state that was hardly more progressive than its southern neighbors? In the mid-1950s Collins vetoed extremist measures proposed by legislative leaders and argued that Florida needed to alter its racial policies because they threatened the state's economic progress and future growth. He pointed out that companies from the North had expressed reluctance to move into the South as long as it remained segregated and violently opposed to desegregation.[1] This argument resonated with many new Floridians and with some natives, who well remembered the state's extended economic depression and who welcomed the post–World War II prosperity.

The strategy of both Collins and Askew was to prevent the forces of resistance and racial alienation from taking control of the state. In 1972, for example, opponents of the use of school busing to achieve desegregation succeeded in having the legislature place a straw ballot before the voters, asking them whether they wanted to amend the U.S. Constitution to prohibit forced busing. Eager to avoid an incident that would isolate Florida from the national mainstream and alienate Floridians from one another, Askew convinced the legislature to add a second item to the same ballot. His measure asked voters whether they favored "equal opportunity for quality education for all children regardless of race, creed, color, or place of residence and opposed a return to a dual system of public schools." Askew then campaigned throughout the state for the second initiative. Although Floridians disliked busing and registered their opposition to it, they overwhelmingly adopted the Askew proposal as well. The governor had not only defused the emotions surrounding racial change but ended any further discussion of segregated education in Florida.[2]

The successful desegregation of Florida demonstrated that political progress requires a special brand of leadership and often a bold approach to public policy. Collins and Askew exercised what might be called "principled pragmatism." Both relied on democratic discourse and voter education to change the political climate without alienating opponents and creating a political backlash. Both saw reasoned discussion and education as essential to their policies.

The same sort of leadership would serve Florida well today. Florida history is littered with sound proposals that failed politically because they were devised behind closed doors without public consent. Some recent examples include the decision to build the Cross-Florida Barge Canal and the "services tax" legislation that was written by lawmakers during a late-night pizza party in 1987. Both occurred with little public discussion and without consideration of the consequences.

The issues confronting the state today are sufficiently complex that citizens have little consensus or understanding about what to do. Florida's political leaders need to consider a number of major policy changes to ensure Florida's prosperity and quality of life for the long term. The state's ability to address its racial past should serve as a model as it seeks to address the needs of its aging population, its ethnic and racial diversity, its environmental needs, and its economic future. Only then will it be successful.

An Environment at Risk

Floridians live in a fragile environment that is threatened annually by hurricanes and daily by humans. The state's historical commitment to growth at almost any cost led to the near destruction of the Everglades and to pollution of the drinking water in South Florida. Damage from the hurricanes has been obvious, while that from humans has been less so, especially to drinking water because it lies in limestone caverns just below the earth's surface. Recognition of the delicate nature of the state's environment has been slow to dawn on policy leaders and citizens, except after hurricanes. Floridians did not begin to understand how truly vulnerable their environment is until they suffered through the droughts of the late 1990s and saltwater intruded into the drinking water of South Florida.

To devise stronger growth management and environmental protection policies, Florida's leaders must deal with rising opposition from landowners, realtors, developers, the housing industry, and others who believe that existing policies have already gone too far. Systematic efforts at environmental protection that began in the 1970s produced a policy framework that is under increasing attack for being heavy-handed, bureaucratic, duplicative, and costly. The failure of environmentalists and state government to consider the concerns of property owners led to a property rights backlash in the late 1980s. Leaders of the movement persuaded state officials to adopt the Private Property Protection Act of 1995, which guarantees compensation for property owners if their development rights are substantially restricted. In a state with a strong populist streak of independence, the property rights movement found resonance with many Floridians.

Shell-shocked by the anger of property rights advocates, state officials found themselves caught between environmental and economic interests. In an effort to salvage environmental protection during this political donnybrook, supporters promoted "sustainable development." Governor Chiles embraced the concept in 1993 and appointed the Commission for a Sustainable South Florida, which was instrumental in securing federal and state agreement on a plan to restore the Everglades. Despite this achievement, many view sustainability as so nebulous and all encompassing that many environmentalists, property owners, and growth advocates are unhappy with it. One aspect of sustainable development seeks to promote ecotourism and similar ecosystem-friendly businesses, but clearly such businesses can never be more than a small part of Florida's economy. Similarly, the "new urbanism," which calls for suburban development to look more like traditional small towns—with broad sidewalks, on-street parking, and mixed residential development—can make urban living more satisfying, but it cannot solve the state's enormous urban growth and resulting urban sprawl.

From a political perspective the problem with Florida's current system of growth management and environmental protection is that it does not offer a reasonable compromise between the environmental movement and the property rights movement, and it has yet to satisfy Floridians. Environmentalists have come to accept the notion that most development must be allowed to proceed if property owners are not to suffer unconstitutional infringements of their rights and have settled for being able to influence the character of new development in order to reduce or mitigate its harmful environmental effects. Conversely, developers have been willing to allow extensive changes in their projects in return for being authorized to proceed. However, this compromise has failed to address the issue of location. As we have noted, the principal weakness of Florida's approach to growth management and environmental protection has been its failure to prevent the intrusion of urbanization into the state's most sensitive ecosystems. Because land-use planning and regulation in Florida have paid less attention to the location of development than to its character and infrastructure, the state has thousands of beautiful developments—manicured neighborhoods, campuslike office parks, self-contained malls, and lush golf courses— that often are located near or atop the state's large water-dependent ecosystems.

If Florida's growth management system is ever going to protect the state's fragile environment, it must cordon off large swaths of environmentally sensitive lands from urbanization and development, and the state must pay for the land or the development rights in question. The state already has the nation's largest program of land acquisition, and it also has a court-tested program—the Area of Critical State Concern (ACSC) program—for designating geographical areas that need special attention. Admittedly, Floridians may not be able to afford all the land that the state should buy to protect its environmental resources. Inevitably, choices will have to be made about which ecosystems are more important to the state's future, and citizens will have to be invested in that decision if it is to have long-term effectiveness. Floridians have come to recognize that growth cannot continue unmanaged, but they have not agreed on how to balance growth and environmental protection and where that balance should be. Florida needs to establish a process that explicitly and fairly balances environmental concerns and property rights. By expanding the ACSC program incrementally and augmenting ACSC designation, Florida could strengthen its protection of large interdependent ecosystems and compensate landowners for their loss of development rights.

Economic Growth and Employment

Policy makers in Florida have found the state's economic condition no less malleable than its environment. The state saw a dramatic shift away from its agricultural roots in the twentieth century as more and more citizens, newcomers, and especially the young moved into other areas of the economy. Florida had 279,370 agricultural workers in 1920, who comprised 28.8 percent of the population. By 1990 the figure had declined to 105,419 and the percentage to just 2.1; both numbers were the lowest in the southeastern United States. The state's massive population growth overwhelmed its land, consuming miles of farmland in the process. Although agriculture remains an important segment of the state's economy, it is not an area of job growth.[3]

The boom in the tourist industry rapidly bypassed agriculture after World War II, as visitors came to enjoy the beaches and subsequently Florida's major entertainment attractions; this shift led the service sector to dominate the economy in the second half of the twentieth century. Policy leaders embraced the tourist industry initially as a way out of a rural existence. But policy makers, like Floridians generally, have never been completely enthralled by the tourist attractions. While they have created an enormous number of jobs and provided greater opportunity, most jobs are low paying and offer limited futures. These so-called dead-end jobs are crucial to this industry and its profitability, but they are not conducive to the long-term economic prosperity of the state's citizens. In an article in a 1997 issue of *Florida Trend Magazine,* a mother bemoaned her and her daughter's experiences in Florida's low-wage economy. She had decided to pursue a university degree when her daughter left home for college. The two graduated at almost the same time, and both were able to find jobs with salaries in the $21,000 to $22,000 range. The mother asked rhetorically why she and her daughter had bothered to attend university if that was all their degrees could command in Florida.[4]

Despite the efforts of political leaders to broaden economic opportunities in the state, the service sector continues to be the fastest-growing area of employment; it is expanding so rapidly that companies rely on immigrants to fill most of these positions, in part because Floridians are unwilling to take such jobs at such low salaries. This trend has led to one of those sub rosa developments that state leaders have avoided discussing, because Florida has, with the exception of Cuban immigrants, actively discouraged immigration from the Caribbean and Central and South America for fear of being overwhelmed by unskilled immigrants. But in the high tourist areas of Florida, nearly all the maids and support personnel in motels and hotels are immigrants or migrant workers from countries in the Americas.

State leaders have sought a variety of approaches to strengthen and diversify the economy in recent years, from major tax breaks to businesses to partnerships with universities. They have looked longingly at the boom in advanced technology companies in California, Massachusetts, North Carolina, and Washington State and have sought ways to start up or lure such companies to Florida. Despite substantial investments, it was not clear until recently that such companies felt they could be compatible with a tourist economy. Some of that now seems to be changing, with technology advancements along the I-4 corridor in Central Florida.

At the same time Florida's leadership has begun to embrace its diversity as a way to enhance its emerging global economy in the Caribbean and Latin America. Miami has become the de facto capital of the region in many ways and the crossroads of the Americas. Sixty percent of Florida's trade is with Latin America, and that trade has been steadily expanding since the early 1990s. Despite recent bumps in the road from the terrorist attacks of September 11, 2001, the economic futures of Miami and Florida have begun to meld into the global marketplace. Florida has three metropolitan areas ranked in the top forty in the United States: Tampa–St. Petersburg is twenty-fifth with $82 billion in goods and services, Miami twenty-ninth with nearly $72 billion, and Orlando thirty-eighth with $60 billion.[5] These developments offer some interesting economic opportunities for the state and its citizens, but they also pose challenges to the state's traditional culture and to relationships between natives and recent immigrants.

The emergence of a global economy and the continued expansion of the service economy in Florida have broadened opportunities for Florida's ethnic and racial minorities. One significant but often overlooked feature of Florida's service-driven economy is the opportunity that it provides for women- and minority-owned firms. Statistics for the years 1980 to 1998 in Florida reveal that the number of black-owned firms ranked fourth nationally, while Hispanic firms ranked third, and women-owned firms ranked fourth.[6] The service economy offers several points of entry for women and minorities that large corporations do not. The global economy also appears to offer the same access, especially to ethnic groups from Latin America.

While these economic developments have lessened racial and ethnic tensions, discrimination persists. Many black businessmen and women have complained about a variety of forms of discrimination that have been only partially offset by their business achievements. And while few Cuban Americans and other Hispanics have encountered overt discrimination, they hear considerable complaints from whites who resent the latinization of their society. Natives grumble frequently, for example, about the widespread use of Spanish in South Florida.

The challenge for policy leaders in the state is to find ways to promote economic advancement while encouraging greater understanding among its racial and ethnic communities. And yet, for the most part, state political leaders have opted to ignore racial and ethnic issues, fearing that their political future may be jeopardized if they speak out. Most support the concept of a global economy and the interests of Cuban Americans, but they generally oppose immigration into Florida from other parts of the Caribbean and Latin America. Only Governor Jeb Bush seems to understand the ways in which these issues intersect, and he has been alone in his willingness to conduct a public dialogue on such matters.

Community Redevelopment and Local Government Reform

As Florida attempts to diversify its economy and promote economic opportunity, it must also address the ghetto-like conditions of many of its African-American neighborhoods. A number of local and regional governments have demonstrated the ability to restructure the business activities and housing patterns of large geographical areas. Fort Lauderdale offers a good example of this. In the 1950s and 1960s the city was the nation's most popular destination for college students on spring break, and the businesses in the beach area focused on this particular clientele. As the surrounding Broward County became more urban and more economically affluent, residents viewed student tourism as less desirable than other forms of development. So in the late 1980s the Fort Lauderdale city council made a conscious decision to transform the beach area into a more fashionable and attractive destination for European tourists. City planners reconfigured the roadways along the beach and worked with hotel and motel owners to help them pool their land, tear down some of the smaller, less successful facilities, and build large hotels more suitable to an upscale clientele. The redevelopment initiative proved enormously successful and completely transformed the face of tourism in Fort Lauderdale in less than a decade.

Many other communities in Florida have reinvented themselves in a similar fashion. Delray Beach, West Palm Beach, and Fort Pierce, for example, have all redeveloped their downtowns to recapture the feel of Old Florida. Miami's South Beach area took another course, becoming a glamorous international nightspot for the rich and the young, after many years as a deteriorating area for poor retirees. Tampa and Jacksonville have redeveloped areas along the waterfront to attract nightlife and tourists. These two cities also recruited national sports teams to add another dimension to their downtown redevelopment. These and many other examples demonstrate that blighted areas of Florida can be resuscitated economically and culturally if city and state leaders are so motivated.

To alleviate conditions in its slums and remove the last remnants of its racist past, Florida needs to make a similar commitment to its minority citizens, especially in those communities along the east and west coasts. The redevelopment of some blight belt communities has been successful in municipalities whose land-use patterns connected the interests of commercial zones or affluent white neighborhoods with the needs and concerns of black residents. In such cases the entire community came together through its municipal political processes to invest resources sufficient to revitalize its poor neighborhoods. Delray Beach, for example, which had been polarized by racial tensions in the early 1990s, invested heavily in neighborhood redevelopment in order to rebuild a sense of community and to reach out to minority citizens.

Such initiatives have not been more common because Florida's system of local government often prevents adequate representation of the interests of impoverished indigenous African Americans in local politics. Frequently, four-lane or six-lane roads, expressways, walls, fences, stadiums, railroad tracks, and other physical barriers separate affluent residential and commercial districts from the blight belt. As a result, the fate of Florida's African-American urban poor often becomes irrelevant to and hidden from the prosperity of the rest of the community. Only when their economic circumstances bear directly on those of the white middle and upper classes, as in Jacksonville, have Florida's black urban poor been able to persuade local governments to address their situation.

As Florida's economy continues its expansion and its society further diversifies, state and local governments would be wise to marshal resources to address the blight of its ghettos, much of which it created with zoning laws, highway construction projects, and racial policies. (Tampa, for example, wants to place its plans for the Olympics in the middle of a poor black community.) In the process Florida should reform its system of local government to give minorities a larger voice. To some extent changes to local electoral systems are inevitable. African Americans and other minorities have repeatedly won in court when they have shown that racial traditions of the past have effectively disfranchised them. Florida would be better off, however, if the state and local communities initiated the changes, rather than waiting for the courts to act. When the courts have acted, judges have mandated that single-member districts replace at-large elections. The consequence of at-large elections has been that the interests of a particular district in communities like Miami, Jacksonville, and West Palm Beach, rather than those of the community as a whole, have dominated local governments. Bringing minorities more fully into the local political process offers the promise of reducing racial tensions while also creating political conditions that will benefit the entire community.

Public Education

No area of public life has been the subject of so much attention or so frustrated policy leaders as public education. Floridians of all stripes, and business leaders especially, complain repeatedly that the shortcomings in the state's educational system have severely limited Florida's economic advancement. In an era of high technology and expanding global trade, businesspeople argue that Florida is being held back by a foundering educational system that leaves many young people with insufficient skills to contribute to this new economy. Educational statistics have underscored their concerns. Florida ranks near the bottom of the nation in the graduation rate of students and among the lowest on student achievement test scores on national examinations; too many students graduate from high school without sufficient writing, mathematical, or analytical skills to move into skilled jobs.

In recent years both the Chiles and Bush administrations pursued similar objectives in their K–12 initiatives. Perturbed by the academic results of the public schools during a period in which the state significantly increased its funding levels, both governors implemented accountability measures to improve educational quality in the state, and the Bush administration added penalties for those schools whose academic results fail to improve over time. Chiles and Bush also sought to bring Florida's public schools into a policy-oriented dialogue with parents, employers, and community leaders. As it stands, parents and the community at large have little if any leverage in school decision making. School administration at the local level is separated from city and county governments, organized as an independent special-purpose district and often administered by an appointed superintendent.

The Chiles administration launched two process-centered initiatives. First, it established a program to organize parents at each school, evaluate school performance on the basis of standardized student testing, and involve parents and educators in a collaborative planning process to raise student achievement. The program also required the testing of teachers for competency in their areas of instruction. While this initiative had some benefits—particularly in developing a standardized process for evaluating student performance in all the state's schools—it did not improve the responsiveness of schools to their surrounding communities.

The other program initiated by the Chiles administration authorized the creation of "charter schools." Operating as private schools, charter schools are eligible to receive public funding equivalent to the per-pupil funding of the public schools. Charter schools have most of the freedoms of private schools: They can hire teachers without having a union contract; they can develop their own methods of instruction; they can operate at a location of their own choosing and in a facility of their own design; and so on. In order to receive public funding charter schools gain approval from the local school board, operate under school board guidelines, and are open to all students in the district. Virtually all administrative power lies at the school level: The principal and other managers can make whatever personnel changes they deem necessary. Charter schools are held accountable to the public through an annual evaluation of their students' performance on standardized tests.

The charter school experiment has achieved mixed results so far. Students' test scores are no better than those for public school students and often worse. Moreover, the creation of charter schools has severely fragmented and racially segmented school districts. In Broward County, for example, affluent, predominantly white residents have established several charter schools that are now maintained by such cities as Pembroke Pines, North Lauderdale, and Coral Springs. These cities have promoted these schools to attract and retain middle- and upperclass families with school-age children. If other cities follow suit, these schools will end up serving only a narrow segment of the population, and other areas in Broward County will be faced with a return to a dual system of education similar to the one that existed during the days of racial segregation, except that this new system would now be divided by class as well as by race.

Jeb Bush's administration has tried a different approach, to reform public education by empowering parents to remove their children from failing schools. In 1998 Bush established the nation's first statewide voucher program, which enabled parents to receive state money for all or part of the cost of sending their children to private schools. The program relies on the school testing and evaluation program initiated by the Chiles administration. Eligibility for vouchers is limited to parents whose children are in the lowest-performing schools, as measured by student achievement scores. The Bush administration also has linked the funding of individual schools to their academic performance.[7]

Despite these major initiatives, Florida continues to rank among the bottom 15 states in the nation in all major educational categories. In 2000/2001, it stood 38th nationally in funding per student (down from 24th in 1990), 35th in the percentage of those over age 25 with a high school diploma (down from 27th in 1989), 37th in the percentage of those over 25 with a college diploma (down from 27th in 1989), and 49th in the high school graduation rate (down from 48th in 1990). The state legislature pledged to eliminate portable classrooms from all public schools in 1998, but they have continued to proliferate. In concluding its report on Florida in the 1990s, the *St. Petersburg Times* wrote, "While Florida's leaders spent much of the decade talking about investing in the future, they spent only enough to accommodate the state's substantial growth." Charles Reed, former chancellor of the State University System, commented more testily about the legislature's mentality toward investing in public education: "We're cheap and we're proud of it."[8]

How, then, are Florida's public schools to be made accountable to the communities that they are supposed to serve? None of the strategies pursued so far has been successful. The Chiles approach of mobilizing parents and community involvement has been unable to counter the resistance of the educational bureaucracy, and the charter school program has caused more disruption than progress. It is too early to tell whether Bush's approach will succeed, but the response from the courts suggests that the governor's initiatives may all be nonstarters if they cannot pass constitutional muster.

Identifying the principal problems with Florida's public schools and resolving them continues to confound even the experts. Most agree that the state has a host of problems that, when combined, would cause educational problems anywhere in the world. The increase in single-parent households and the high rate of poverty among such families, experts note, undermines educational support for children at home and parental involvement in the schools. Middle- and upper-class children traditionally do well in school, because they receive strong encouragement and support from their parents at home and have many other advantages associated with their parents' income.

The high rate of mobility in Florida has compounded the educational challenges facing the state. Children come and go from schools as parents relocate, leaving teachers struggling to integrate new arrivals into their classrooms, only to find them leaving again three months later. In 1995–96 an examination of the Miami-Dade school district, the nation's fourth biggest and Florida's largest, most diverse, and perhaps most dynamic system, suggested the magnitude of the problem. In that school year 42,000 students moved into the district, 39,000 students moved within the school system, and 34,000 moved out of the system. The lack of stability in the system created havoc in the classroom, where teachers struggled from day to day to help their students advance academically.[9]

The growing size and increasing diversity of the student body also complicates the educational process in Florida. During the 1990s new Floridians—from northern states, Latin America, and the Caribbean—added more than 600,000 students, many of whom arrived without English language skills, to the state's sixty-seven school districts. As educators describe it, Florida is adding the equivalent of a 60,000-student district, with students from throughout the nation and Latin America, to the state public school roster each year. Public school enrollment swelled from 1.7 million students in 1987 to 2.3 million students in 1998–99, and a slowdown is not expected until the 2003–4 school year. Florida is home to seven of the nation's twenty-five largest school districts and some of the most ethnically and racially diverse. These include the counties of Miami-Dade, Broward, Hillsborough, Orange, Palm Beach, Duval, and Pinellas.

At the same time school bureaucracies pump millions of dollars into office buildings for administrators but leave teachers without critical supplies and books for classroom teaching and pull top teachers out of the classroom to become administrators. And on the other side, teachers' unions balk at merit pay for outstanding teachers and for those in critical need areas and generally resist reform proposals that seek to raise accountability standards for teachers and schools.

A 1998 survey by the James Madison Institute and the Collins Center for Public Policy, two leading public policy institutes in Florida, confirmed that education is the top priority of Floridians and that school overcrowding, safety and discipline, quality of teaching, and academic performance are the major areas of concern. The survey further revealed that Floridians are willing to invest more money in their public schools, but they also want to experiment with alternatives, such as school choice, in an effort to improve the educational results.[10]

There are no easy answers to Florida's educational malaise. There clearly need to be systematic efforts to improve public education, including additional funding but also teacher and parent accountability and parent and community involvement in the educational process. The worst thing Florida can do is settle for the educational solution of the day, but that is precisely what it has done since the 1970s. Bush has recently instituted broadbased reforms by linking performance with funding and integrating all public education, K–20, into one seamless system. But the results of these changes are by no means clear, and it is significant that no other state has yet seen the wisdom of following Florida's lead.

Caring for the Frail Elderly

Despite general recognition that the state's senior population will soar in the near future, Floridians have yet to come to grips with the consequences of this development for medical care and support services for the elderly. Having large numbers of seniors who live well into their frail years is a relatively new situation for the state and one that will expand dramatically in the coming decades. Historically, older retirees have returned home to be cared for by their children. This situation promises to change in the future as more and more seniors have children who live in Florida.

An aging population will require many more nursing homes unless the state develops alternative solutions. If Florida only offers nursing homes to care for its aging seniors, the state will quickly run out of both money and facilities. The only way Florida can support a substantial senior population without going broke is to develop services and support systems that allow retirees to live independently for as long as possible. Moreover, the evidence strongly suggests that seniors prefer to maintain their independence as long as they can, and generally they live longer and healthier lives when they do.

Aging in place, as it is called, will nevertheless impose certain burdens that require the state's undivided attention. In particular, the responsibility for caring for the elderly will fall on friends and relatives living nearby. This can be an enormous burden for children and even more so for neighbors. Typically, the children of seniors are in the most productive years of their lives, have children of their own that they are trying to assist, and are beginning to plan for retirement themselves. When a parent or parents suddenly require more attention, the adult child is often unprepared and finds the financial responsibilities overwhelming. Neighbors are not in any better position to care for seniors, and they lack the familial connection and often the resources to do so. Florida needs to examine ways to assist these caregivers so that they can provide support without suffering burnout and without going broke. Sarasota's Senior Friendship Center offers one possible approach by providing a wide variety of programs for seniors while also offering a medical clinic, staffed by retired doctors and nurses under the Public Health Service, to care for the indigent elderly.

As the lives of Americans increasingly extend beyond the centenary mark, more serious ailments, from the loss of sight and hearing to serious physical decline, will increase and the difficulty of caring for seniors will be compounded. It is impossible at this point to say what the public and private sectors will need to do to help Floridians adapt to these new circumstances, but it is demonstrably clear that a wider range of services will be essential. Florida's political leaders need to guide citizens in a public discussion about retirement, aging, and parental care so that these issues do not descend on the state and its citizens all at once. To the extent that Florida's residents are prepared to handle the responsibilities of aging, the public expense and the burden will be reduced, and aging will be seen as a natural part of the life cycle in which all Floridians share responsibly.

Florida's Children

Almost lost in these demographic changes and their significance for the state's future have been Florida's children. During the 1990s Florida's teenage population grew at a rate—35 percent—that exceeded that for seniors—18 percent. Florida's 3.6 million teens place the state fourth behind California, Texas, and New York, and their population is larger than the teen population of all six New England states combined (see table 11).

Projections through 2020 are that the teenage population will continue to expand in Florida, reaching over 4 million. As a proportion of the population, Florida's child and youth population was the second highest nationally (behind only Nevada's) from 1985 to 2001. Moreover, between 2000 and 2015, the number of teenagers and young adults (those aged fourteen to twenty-four) is expected to increase by 23 percent.[11] Concerns about the graying of Florida have masked these statistics. and few Floridians are aware of them.

In the rush to address the needs of seniors, Florida's political leaders literally lost sight of the needs of the state's children. In 1994, Florida ranked near the bottom among the fifty states in a host of categories dealing with the well-being of children. From death rates for children (ranked eighth) to violent death rates for teens (ranked fourth) to arrest rates for juveniles (ranked third), Florida children and teenagers seemed to be a generation in crisis. The poverty figures for and health needs of these children further underscored this dismal picture. Florida ranked seventh nationally for children in extreme poverty and seventh for the number of children without health insurance. Added to these statistics, the state ranked third in the rate of single-parent families, first in the rate of high-school dropouts, fourth for teenagers not in school and not working, and fifth for the number of children living in high dropout neighborhoods.[12]

In 1995, the Chiles administration invested heavily in the Healthy Start, Healthy Kids, and Healthy Family initiatives, and the Bush administration has continued to do so. According to the *2000 National Kids Count Data Book*, Florida now ranks thirty-fifth in the nation on a composite of ten key indicators of child health, family security, edu-

Table 11. Florida's teenage population

Year	Teenage population	Total population
1970	831,235	6,789,443
1980	1,093,617	9,746,324
1990	1,088,827	12,937,926
2000	3,646,340	15,982,378

cation, and youth well-being, up from fortieth in 1995 and from forty-eighth in 1994. But the state can take little pride in its standing among other states because it ranks below the national average in seven of the ten indicators. Moreover, Florida's per capita income ranks nineteenth in the nation, making the gap between its ranking in the *National Kids Count Data Book* and its per capita income the largest in the nation.[13]

Whether one uses the most recent statistics regarding children or earlier ones, the numbers suggest that Florida's inability to protect its children may well produce an adult generation that will experience a host of social and economic problems. The social trends shaping these statistics for children have been in place for more than two decades, which means that such developments cannot be turned around quickly even if the state chose to invest more heavily in the Healthy Start Program for children and add new programs focusing on children's needs. And yet, as we write, the 2000 legislature imposed cuts in these programs to meet the Republican goal of reducing the size of government.

Among the nation's fifty largest cities, Miami has the third highest percentage of children (38 percent) living in extremely impoverished neighborhoods, and many of these children live in single-parent households. They are often passed from one relative to another, or the parent moves frequently to find better employment. Although many in the Miami-Dade business community see the education system as a major impediment to economic growth and the economic future of the city, the data suggest that the problem is much more complex.

Will the Baby Boomers allow political leaders to address the needs of other age groups, especially the young? U.S. senator Bob Graham recently commented, "Elders bring energy, vitality, and wisdom to the community."[14] But can and will they mobilize that energy, vitality, and wisdom to support state programs to enhance schools, to mentor children, and to develop new programs to meet the needs of children? Florida will have a great human resource in its seniors, but that resource will have little consequence if it stays confined to gated communities and ignores the realities of the world outside them.

Crime and Teenagers

A number of experts have contended that Florida's juvenile crime statistics are directly related to the social disintegration of the family. Others counter that the crime statistics more accurately reflect the state's highly dynamic population: People without ties to any community drift through Florida and commit a high proportion of these crimes. Whichever side is correct may not matter much. Crime undermines social stability and confidence in the future and discourages businesses from locating to Florida.

Florida's arrest rate for juveniles involved in violent crime—homicide, forcible rape, robbery, or aggravated assault per 100,000 children aged ten to seventeen—stood among the highest in the nation in 1995, surpassed only by Pennsylvania, New York, and the District of Columbia. The criminologist James Alan Fox, writing about the dramatic rise in juvenile crime, warned in 1995, "Unless we act today, we're going to have a bloodbath when these kids grow up." Between 1985 and 1995 the rate at which teens aged fourteen to seventeen murdered people rose 165 percent. The *New York Times* warned that if this trend continues, "the number will double by the year 2010."[15]

Significantly, the projections were revised downward as the state and national economies improved dramatically from 1992 to 2000. Youth violence, as evidenced by the shootings at Columbine High School and elsewhere, remains alarming, but, as with all other crimes, it declined during this period. Suddenly, the public fear that made crime prevention the number one priority among Floridians in the first half of the decade fell to fifth place in 1999. What remains distressing is the high percentage of young criminals who are African American. Currently 48 percent of all those in Florida's prisons are black.[16]

As youth crime peaked, experts began to express their reservations about the treatment of youth offenders. Is incarceration the answer? they asked. One study estimated that society more than benefits in dollar terms and in the general feeling of safety from the incarceration of youthful criminals who commit murder, assault, and robbery. For less serious youth crimes, however, sociologists and criminologists in North America, Europe, Australia, and New Zealand have called for an entirely new framework—restorative justice—that elevates the role of crime victims and holds offenders directly accountable to the people and communities that they have violated. The restorative justice, or "public shaming," approach seeks accountability and an understanding of the seriousness of these youthful transgressions, without locking the youth away with more serious offenders for long periods of time. Whether this sort of "public shaming" will be more effective and acceptable to citizens as a device to reduce juvenile crime remains to be seen.[17]

Surveys of judges, state attorneys, and public defenders in Florida reveal that delinquency prevention and intervention is their top priority. Despite the decline in crime, officials recognize that the rate of crimes by youthful offenders is likely to remain high and that only proactive measures will ensure its reduction. Studies of criminal activity point out that most crime is committed by males aged fifteen to twenty-eight. Recently, a team of sociologists documented that locking juveniles away with more serious adult offenders has been counterproductive: The young offenders become more likely to commit more serious, violent crimes upon their release than when they first entered prison.[18] For these reasons the team proposed delinquency prevention and intervention as the cornerstones of a crime prevention program. Their second recommendation was the provision of education and rehabilitation for the incarcerated, recognizing that many youthful offenders will eventually be paroled as adults and will need to have some education and skills to ensure that they find legitimate work once released. These reforms have yet to win endorsement from state politicians. For now they are content to lock juveniles away and have developed few programs and allocated few public resources for rehabilitation.

A Final Observation

While Florida faces substantial pressures that could derail its progress in the twenty-first century, it also has an opportunity to be a leader among the states and an international leader in the Caribbean and Latin America. Solutions to such matters as the graying of Florida, racial and ethnic diversity, environmental protection, education, global trade, and the provision of programs for children and young people are pivotal and will define the state's place in this century. The challenges are substantial, both individually and collectively, and they raise the question of whether Florida has the political maturity and leadership to address these issues. For now, we must stay tuned.

Notes

Introduction

1. *New York Times*, April 8, 1999, 1A.
2. *Florida Agriculturalist*, January 19, 1881. Also quoted in Mohl and Pozzetta, "From Migration to Multiculturalism," 392.
3. *New York Times*, June 7, 1999, 16A; November 11, 1999, 8A; November 12, 1999, 22A; February 4, 2000, 1A; March 6, 2000, 14A.

Chapter 1. The Evolution of Florida to 1940

1. Colburn and deHaven-Smith, *Government in the Sunshine State*, 8–9.
2. Ibid., 15.
3. Ibid., 19–20.
4. Rogers, "Fortune and Misfortune," 291–92.
5. See Foster, *Castles in the Sand*, 164–65, 166, 207, 214.
6. Rogers, "Great Depression," 287–303.
7. Gannon, *Florida: A Short History*, 82.
8. Colburn and Scher, *Florida's Gubernatorial Politics*, 190–92.
9. Blake, *Land into Water*, 157.

Chapter 2. World War II and the Modernization of Florida

1. Mormino, "World War II," 325.
2. *Miami Herald*, May 7, 1985. Also cited in Mormino, "World War II," 337.
3. Mormino, "World War II," 325.
4. Colburn and Scher, *Florida's Gubernatorial Politics*, 205–6.
5. Ibid., 244–45.
6. Lawson, Colburn, and Paulson, "Groveland," 315–20. Also in "Florida's Little Scottsboro Case," 25–26.
7. Colburn and deHaven-Smith, *Government in the Sunshine State*, 33.
8. Colburn and Scher, *Florida's Gubernatorial Politics*, 175.
9. Wagy, *Governor LeRoy Collins*, 136.
10. The Supreme Court case was *Swann v. Adams*, 385 U.S. 440 (1967).
11. Mohl and Pozzetta, "From Migration to Multiculturalism," 405.

Chapter 3. A Changing Population and a Changing Florida

1. Blake, *Land into Water*, 196–212.
2. Ibid., 227–30; also see Colburn and Scher, *Florida's Gubernatorial Politics*, 217–18.
3. *St. Petersburg Times*, September 12, 1990, 20; MacKay, "Florida's Crowd."
4. Gannon, *Florida: A Short History*, 143.
5. Colburn and deHaven-Smith, "Florida," 15.
6. Ibid., 15–17.
7. Colburn and deHaven-Smith, *Government in the Sunshine*, 75.
8. Delaney, "Governing at the Local Level," 8.
9. *St. Petersburg Times*, October 4, 2001, 8.

Chapter 4. A View of the Twenty-first Century in Florida

1. deHaven-Smith, "Leadership Florida 1999 Statewide Survey."
2. Colburn and deHaven-Smith, "Demographics of Florida," 1.
3. Massey, "New Immigration and Ethnicity," 643.
4. Frey, "Minority Magnet Metros in the 1990s."
5. *New York Times*, January 6, 2000, 16A; April 1, 2000, 1A; April 26, 2000, 1A.
6. MacManus, "Aging in Florida," 9.
7. Ambrose, *Citizen Soldiers*, 472.
8. MacManus, "Aging in Florida," 8–9, 18.
9. Ibid., 8.
10. Ibid.

Chapter 5. The Impending Battle over Florida's Future

1. Colburn and deHaven-Smith, *Government in the Sunshine State*, 73.
2. Chads are small, square, numbered perforations associated with the names of candidates on the cardboard sheets used as ballots in the punched card system.
3. Final Report, Governor's Select Task Force on Election Procedures, Standards and Technology (Tallahassee, 2001). For its report the task force updated data from a survey by the *Orlando Sentinel* of all sixty-seven county elections supervisors in Florida. The newspaper published the results on November 14, 2000.
4. *Washington Post*, January 28, 2001, 2.
5. Ibid., January 28–February 4, 2001.
6. See Carter, *Florida Experience*; DeGrove, *Land, Growth, and Politics*.
7. See Clark, "Sources of Revenue."
8. *St. Petersburg Times*, March 4, 2001, 1A; March 8, 2001, 1A.

Chapter 6. The Political Challenges of the Twenty-first Century

1. Colburn and Scher, *Florida's Gubernatorial Politics*, 231–32.

2. Ibid., 228–30.

3. Nevertheless, farming remains an important segment of the state's economy, even if it is less visible today than it was fifty years ago. Farm income in 1992, for example, totaled more than $6 billion, ranking the state tenth in the nation. Much of Florida's agricultural income is generated through crop production, including citrus, where the state ranks fourth nationally. Florida remains the second largest producer of citrus in the world, behind Brazil.

4. *Florida Trend*, August 1997.

5. *Orlando Sentinel*, July 11, 2001, 1A, 8A.

6. Bureau of Economic and Business Research, *Florida and the Nation*, 101–4.

7. See Collins Center, "School Choice."

8. *St. Petersburg Times*, November 14, 2001, 5B.

9. Colburn and deHaven-Smith, "Demographics of Florida," 5.

10. Pritchett, "School Choice." The survey was actually conducted in the summer of 1998 by Dresner, Wickers, and Associates with a margin of error of plus or minus 4 percent.

11. Bureau of Economic and Business Research, *Florida and the Nation*.

12. Ibid.

13. *Gainesville Sun*, May 22, 2001, 1. Also see Annie E. Casie Foundation, "National Composite Rank, 1998."

14. Graham, "Florida as a Laboratory," 6.

15. *New York Times*, September 8, 1995, 16A.

16. *Orlando Sentinel*, July 25, 2001, 1.

17. Umbreit, "Holding Juvenile Offenders Accountable."

18. Bishop et al., "Transfer of Juveniles to Criminal Court."

Bibliography

Ambrose, Stephen E. *Citizen Soldiers: The U.S. Army from the Normandy Beaches to the Bulge to the Surrender of Germany June 7, 1944–May 7, 1945*. New York: Simon & Schuster, 1997.

Annie E. Casie Foundation. "National Composite Rank, 1998." *2001 Kids County Data Book Online*. http://www.aecf.org/kidscount/kc2000/ (September 4, 2001).

Arsenault, Raymond. "The End of the Long Hot Summer: The Air-Conditioner and Southern Culture." *Journal of Southern History* 6, no. 4 (November 1984): 597–628.

———. *St. Petersburg and the Florida Dream, 1888–1950*. Norfolk, Va.: Donning, 1988.

Bernard, Richard M., and Bradley R. Rice, eds. *Sunbelt Cities: Politics and Growth Since World War II*. Austin: University of Texas Press, 1983.

Bishop, Donna M., Charles E. Frazier, Lonn Lanza-Kaduce, and Lawrence Winner. "The Transfer of Juveniles to Criminal Court: Does It Make a Difference?" *Crime & Delinquency* 42, no. 2 (April 1996): 171–91.

Blake, Nelson M. *Land into Water—Water into Land: A History of Water Management in Florida*. Tallahassee: Florida State University Press, 1980.

Bouvier, Leon F., and Bob Weller. *Florida in the Twenty-first Century: The Challenge of Population Growth*. Washington, D.C.: Center for Immigration Studies, 1992.

Bureau of Economic and Business Research. *Florida and the Nation, 1998*. 2d ed. Gainesville: Bureau of Economic and Business Research, Warrington College of Business Administration, University of Florida, June 1998.

———. *Florida Statistical Abstract*. Gainesville: Bureau of Economic and Business Research, Warrington College of Business Administration, University of Florida. Various years.

Button, James. *Blacks and Social Change: Impact of the Civil Rights Movement in Southern Communities*. Princeton, N.J.: Princeton University Press, 1989.

Carr, Patrick. *Sunshine States: Wild Times and Extraordinary Lives in the Land of Gators, Guns, and Grapefruits*. 1990. Reprint, Gainesville: University Press of Florida, 1999.

Carter, Arthur J. *The Florida Experience: Land and Water Policy in a Growth State*. Baltimore: Johns Hopkins University Press, 1974.

Cash, William T. *A History of the Democratic Party in Florida*. Tallahassee: Florida Democratic Historical Foundation, 1936.

Chalmers, David. "The Ku Klux Klan in the Sunshine State: The 1920s." *Florida Historical Quarterly* 42, no. 3 (January 1964): 209–15.

Clark, Wayne A. "Sources of Revenue and Managing Growth." In *Growth Management Innovations in Florida*, ed. Westi Jo deHaven-Smith. 73–88. Ft. Lauderdale: Florida Atlantic University and Florida International University Joint Center for Environmental and Urban Problems, 1988.

Colburn, David R. *Racial Change and Community Crisis: St. Augustine, Florida, 1877–1980*. 1985. Reprint, Gainesville: University Press of Florida, 1991.

Colburn, David R., and Lance deHaven-Smith. "The Demographics of Florida." Paper prepared for the 1999 Meeting of the Reubin O'D. Askew Institute on Politics and Society, Gainesville, February 4–6.

———. "Florida: Its Future and the Role of Senior Citizens." In *The Graying of Florida*, 15–17. Report of the 2000 Meeting of the Reubin O'D. Askew Institute on Politics and Society, Gainesville, February 3–5.

———. *Government in the Sunshine State: Florida Since Statehood*. Gainesville: University Press of Florida, 1999.

Colburn, David R., and Jane L. Landers, eds. *The African-American Heritage of Florida*. Gainesville: University Press of Florida, 1995.

Colburn, David R., and Richard K. Scher, *Florida's Gubernatorial Politics in the Twentieth Century*. Gainesville: University Presses of Florida, 1980.

Collins Center for Public Policy. "School Choice: A Rising Sun or Rising Storm on Florida's Horizon?" Collins Center for Public Policy, Tallahassee, 1998.

Dauer, Manning, ed. *Florida's Politics and Government*. Gainesville: University Presses of Florida, 1980.

DeGrove, John M. *Land, Growth, and Politics*. Washington, D.C.: Planners Press, American Planning Association, 1984.

deHaven-Smith, Lance. *Environmental Concern in Florida and the Nation*. Gainesville: University Presses of Florida, 1989.

———. "The Leadership Florida 1999 Statewide Survey: Floridians' Subjective Attachment to the State." Unpublished paper written for Leadership Florida, Tallahassee, 1999.

Delaney, John. "Governing at the Local Level." In *A View of the Twenty-first Century: Demographic Developments and Their Implications for Florida's Future*, 8. Report of the 1999 Meeting of the Reubin O'D. Askew Institute on Politics and Society, Gainesville, February 4–6.

Douglas, Marjory Stoneman. *The Everglades: River of Grass*. New York: Rinehart, 1947.

Dye, Thomas R. *Public Policy in Florida: A Fifty-State Perspective.* Tallahassee: Policy Sciences Program, Florida State University, 1992.

Fiedler, Tom, and Lance deHaven-Smith. *Almanac of Florida Politics, 1998.* Dubuque, Iowa: Kendall/Hunt, 1997.

Fjellman, Stephen M. *Vinyl Leaves: Walt Disney World and America.* Boulder, Colo.: Westview, 1992.

Floyd, Susan S., ed. *Florida Statistical Abstract 1997.* 31st ed. Gainesville: Bureau of Economic and Business Research, Warrington College of Business Administration, University of Florida, 1997.

Flynt, Wayne. *Cracker Messiah: Governor Sidney J. Catts of Florida.* Baton Rouge: Louisiana State University Press, 1977.

————. *Duncan Upshaw Fletcher: Dixie's Reluctant Progressive.* Tallahassee: Florida State University Press, 1971.

Foster, Mark S. *Castles in the Sand: The Life and Times of Carl Graham Fisher.* Gainesville: University Press of Florida, 2000.

Franklin, John Hope. *From Slavery to Freedom: A History of Negro Americans.* 4th ed. New York: Knopf, 1974.

Frey, William H. "Minority Magnet Metros in the 1990s." *Research Report* (July 1998); 98–418. Available from the University of Michigan, Ann Arbor 48104.

Gannon, Michael V. *Florida: A Short History.* Gainesville: University Press of Florida, 1993.

————, ed. *The New History of Florida.* Gainesville: University Press of Florida, 1996.

Graham, Bob. "Florida as a Laboratory for the 21st Century." In *The Graying of Florida,* 6–7. Report of the 2000 Meeting of the Reubin O'D. Askew Institute on Politics and Society, Gainesville, February 3–5.

Hall, Kermit L., and James W. Ely Jr., eds. *An Uncertain Tradition: Constitutionalism and the History of the South.* Athens: University of Georgia Press, 1989.

Havard, William C., and Loren P. Beth. *The Politics of Misrepresentation: Rural-Urban Conflict in the Florida Legislature.* Baton Rouge: Louisiana State University Press, 1962.

Huckshorn, Robert J., ed. *Government and Politics in Florida.* 2d ed. Gainesville: University Press of Florida, 1998.

Ingalls, Robert P. *Urban Vigilantes in the New South: Tampa, 1881–1936.* 1988. Reprint, Gainesville: University Press of Florida, 1993.

Kallina, Edward. *Claude Kirk and the Politics of Confrontation.* Gainesville: University Press of Florida, 1993.

Kersey, Harry A. Jr. *The Florida Seminoles and the New Deal, 1933–1942.* Gainesville: University Presses of Florida, 1989.

Key, V. O., Jr. *Southern Politics in State and Nation.* New York: Vintage, 1949.

Kluger, Richard. *Simple Justice: The History of* Brown v. Board of Education *and Black America's Struggle for Equality.* New York: Knopf, 1976.

Kousser, J. Morgan. *The Shaping of Southern Politics: Suffrage Restriction and the Establishment of the One-Party South, 1880–1910.* New Haven: Yale University Press, 1974.

Lawson, Steven. *Black Ballots: Voting Rights in the South, 1944–1969.* New York: Columbia University Press, 1976.

Lawson, Steven F., David R. Colburn, and Darryl Paulson. "Groveland: Florida's Little Scottsboro." In *African-American Heritage of Florida*, ed. David R. Colburn and Jane L. Landers, 298–325. Gainesville: University Press of Florida, 1995.

McGovern, James R. *Anatomy of a Lynching: The Killing of Claude Neal.* Baton Rouge: Louisiana State University Press, 1982.

MacKay, Buddy. "Florida's Crowd Must Now Become a Community." *St. Petersburg Times*, October 2, 1991, 2.

MacManus, Susan. "Aging in Florida and Its Implications." In *The Graying of Florida*, 8–9, 18. Report of the 2000 Meeting of the Reubin O'D. Askew Institute on Politics and Society, Gainesville, February 3–5.

———. "Retiree Recruitment: How Florida's Burgeoning Senior Population Is Transforming State and Local Politics." *Responses to an Aging Florida* 1, no. 1 (Fall 1998): 12–14.

———. *Young Versus Old: Generational Combat in the Twenty-first Century.* Boulder, Colo.: Westview, 1996.

Massey, Douglas S. "The New Immigration and Ethnicity in the United States in Data and Perspectives." *Population and Development Review* 21, no. 3 (September 1995): 631–52.

Miller, Randall M., and George E. Pozzetta, eds. *Shades of the Sunbelt: Essays on Ethnicity, Race, and the Urban South.* 1988. Reprint, Gainesville: University Press of Florida, 1989.

Mohl, Raymond A. "Miami: The Ethnic Cauldron." In *Sunbelt Cities: Politics and Growth since World War II*, ed. Richard M. Bernard and Bradley R. Rice, 58–99.

———. "Race and Space in the Modern City: Interstate 95 and the Black Community in Miami." In *Urban Policy in Twentieth-Century America*, ed. Arnold R. Hirsch and Raymond A. Mohl, 100–158. New Brunswick, N.J.: Rutgers University Press, 1993.

———, ed. *Searching for the Sunbelt: Historical Perspectives on a Region.* Knoxville: University of Tennessee Press, 1990.

Mohl, Raymond A., and Gary Mormino. "The Big Change in the Sunshine State: A Social History of Modern Florida." In *The New History of Florida*, ed. Michael Gannon, 418–47. Gainesville: University Press of Florida, 1996.

Mohl, Raymond A., and George E. Pozzetta. "From Migration to Multi-culturalism: A History of Florida Immigration." In *The New History of Florida*, ed. Michael Gannon, 391–417. Gainesville: University Press of Florida, 1996.

Mormino, Gary R. "G.I. Joe Meets Jim Crow: Racial Violence and Reform in World War II Florida." *Florida Historical Quarterly* 73, no. 1 (July 1994): 23–42.

———. "World War II." In Gannon, *New History of Florida*, pp. 323–43.

Mormino, Gary R., and George E. Pozzetta. *The Immigrant World of Ybor City: Italians and Their Latin Neighbors in Tampa, 1885–1985*. Urbana: University of Illinois Press, 1987.

Morris, Allen. *The Florida Handbook, 1997–1998*. Tallahassee: Peninsular Publishing, 1997.

Naisbitt, John. *Megatrends: Ten Directions Transforming Our Lives*. New York: Warner, 1982.

Nolan, David. *Fifty Feet in Paradise: The Booming of Florida*. New York: Harcourt Brace Jovanovich, 1984.

Portes, Alejandro, and Alex Stepick. *City on the Edge: The Transformation of Miami*. Berkeley: University of California Press, 1993.

Price, Hugh. *The Negro and Southern Politics: A Chapter of Florida History*. New York: New York University Press, 1957.

Pritchett, Mark. "School Choice: A Rising Sun or Rising Storm?" *Journal of the James Madison Institute*, no. 5 (January–February 1999): 11–16.

Proctor, Samuel. *Napoleon Bonaparte Broward: Florida's Fighting Democrat*. 1950. Reprint, Gainesville: University Press of Florida, 1993.

Richardson, Joe M. *The Negro in the Reconstruction of Florida, 1865–1877*. Tallahassee: Florida State University Press, 1965.

Rogers, William W. "Fortune and Misfortune: The Paradoxical Twenties." In *The New History of Florida*, ed. Michael Gannon, 287–303. Gainesville: University Press of Florida, 1996.

———. "The Great Depression." In *The New History of Florida*, ed. Michael Gannon, 304–22. Gainesville: University Press of Florida, 1996.

———. *Outposts on the Gulf: Saint George Island and Apalachicola from Early Exploration to World War II*. Gainesville: University Presses of Florida, 1986.

Shofner, Jerrell H. "Custom, Law, and History: The Enduring Influence of Florida's `Black Code.'" *Florida Historical Quarterly* 57, no. 3 (January 1977): 277–98.

———. "Florida and Black Migration." *Florida Historical Quarterly* 57, no. 3 (January 1979): 267–88.

———. *Nor Is It Over Yet: Florida in the Era of Reconstruction, 1865–1877*. Gainesville: University Presses of Florida, 1974.

Smith, Charles U., ed. *The Civil Rights Movement in Florida and the United States.* Tallahassee: Father and Son Publishing, 1993.

Tebeau, Charlton W. *A History of Florida.* 1971; rev. ed., Coral Gables: University of Miami Press, 1980.

Tindall, George B. *The Emergence of the New South, 1913–1945.* Baton Rouge: Louisiana State University Press, 1967.

Umbreit, Mark S. "Holding Juvenile Offenders Accountable: A Restorative Justice Perspective." *Juvenile and Family Court Journal* 46, no. 2 (Spring 1995): 31–42.

Vance, Linda D. *May Mann Jennings, Florida's Genteel Activist.* Gainesville: University Presses of Florida, 1980.

Wagy, Thomas R. *Governor LeRoy Collins: Spokesman of the New South.* Tuscaloosa: University of Alabama Press, 1985.

Index

Note: page references in *italics* indicate photographs.

David R. Colburn, provost of the University of Florida, is a professor of history at the University of Florida and executive director of the Reubin O'D. Askew Institute on Politics and Society. He has served as chairman of the Department of History and director of the Institute on American Culture. He has published thirteen books, including *The African-American Heritage of Florida* (UPF, 1995), and coauthored, with deHaven-Smith, *Government in the Sunshine State* (UPF, 1999).

Lance deHaven-Smith is director of the Reubin O'D. Askew Institute on Politics and Society, executive director of the Local Government Commission II, and a professor of public policy at Florida State University. His publications include *The Florida Voter* (Florida Institute of Government, 1995) and *Environmental Concern in Florida and the Nation* (UPF, 1991).